P9-CDW-040

Pope Francis

I BELIEVE

The Promise of the Creed

Edited by Stefan v. Kempis

Translation of German Texts by Robert A. Krieg

Maryknoll, New York 10545

Founded in 1970, Orbis Books endeavors to publish works that enlighten the mind, nourish the spirit, and challenge the conscience. The publishing arm of the Maryknoll Fathers and Brothers, Orbis seeks to explore the global dimensions of the Christian faith and mission, to invite dialogue with diverse cultures and religious traditions, and to serve the cause of reconciliation and peace. The books published reflect the views of their authors and do not represent the official position of the Maryknoll Society. To learn more about Maryknoll and Orbis Books, please visit our website at www.maryknollsociety.org.

First published as Papst Franziskus, *Credo: Was uns das Glaubensbekenntnis verspricht.* Compilation and commentary © Verlag Katholisches Bibelwerk GmbH, Stuttgart 2015.

Published by Orbis Books, Box 302, Maryknoll, NY 10545-0302.

Manufactured in the United States of America

Library of Congress Cataloging-in-Publication

Names: Francis, Pope, 1936- author. | Kempis, Stefan von, 1970- editor.
Title: I believe / Pope Francis ; edited by Stefan v. Kempis ; translation of German texts by Robert A. Krieg.
Other titles: Credo Was uns das Glaubensbekenntinis verspricht. English
Description: Maryknoll : Orbis Books, 2016.
Identifiers: LCCN 2016005548 (print) | LCCN 2016007192 (ebook) | ISBN 9781626981881 (cloth) | ISBN 9781608336746 (ebook)
Subjects: LCSH: Apostles' Creed. | Catholic Church—Doctrines. | Francis, Pope, 1936-
Classification: LCC BT993.3 .F7413 2016 (print) | LCC BT993.3 (ebook) | DDC 238/.11—dc23
LC record available at http://lccn.loc.gov/2016005548

Contents

Introduction

Stefan v. Kempis

What does the Apostles' Creed promise us? That is, to put it in a somewhat more provocative way, would the right confession of faith, the correct creed, bring us somehow a sure advantage, such as more money and success in this life, or at least a higher place in heaven? Some of the free-church groups of Latin America, the home of the new pope, answer yes to this question. However, Francis does not. What therefore does the Creed promise us, and, according to Francis, what can we hope for or anticipate because of our confession of faith?

According to the pope, we can hope not for a prize at life's end but for a way forward in this life. A way that does not lead us in circles but gives a direction in life. Moreover, a way on which we are not alone, for God goes with us. "Whoever has faith is never alone," Francis's predecessor Benedict XVI stated with gentle succinctness. And the Argentinian pope has made these words his own in his first encyclical, *Lumen Fidei* (June 29, 2013). The words correspond in fact to Pope Francis's deepest conviction. In one of the pastoral letters written when he was in Buenos Aires, he said: "The goal, the determining thing, is the encounter with God, with whom we have already entered into communion."

Christian faith is a way forward—an open door, as Francis noted when he was archbishop in Argentina. This view coincides with a dynamic understanding of the Creed, an understanding similar to that of Joseph Ratzinger in his *Introduction to the Christian Faith* (1968), which he wrote during his early years as a professor. In that book, Ratzinger spoke of the Apostles' Creed as inviting not a rigid recitation but a conversation, a dialogue that begins at baptism. Francis makes similar statements but with an entirely different emphasis. Differing from Ratzinger-Benedict, Bergoglio-Francis reasons not on the basis of dogma but on the strong Jesuit spirituality that proceeds from his reflection on actual life. For him, reflection on the Creed entails not precise, comprehensive formulations but illustrative ones. That is, it relies on statements that open, move, lead forward. His form of speech appeals first of all not to the head but to the heart and the imagination.

For this pope, the Christian faith is not a set of doctrines. It is also not some precious item that we must somehow lock away. Christ knocks on the door of our hearts—not from the outside, but from within. On one occasion, the pope preached to the members of his order that Jesuits should be individuals with minds that are open. What matters is unending thinking, oriented to what is new. This orientation is not just a matter of being dynamic and spontaneous. It touches on one's image of God. For the pope, even God is always new: a God of surprises. We believe not in a text but in a person.

This approach does not relativize the Apostle's Creed. However, it does radically prevent us from being satisfied with our understanding of the text. An approach like this also allows us to make the Creed entirely personal. It is no accident that on one occasion this pope as a young adult drafted an entirely personal creed, which attests to the incarnation of the words "I believe" in his own life. The Creed is not chiseled into stone; rather, it is translated into one's life.

In this regard, Francis calls our attention to the fact that it is not only Christians but all people who are making their way through life. We are a great community on the road, and we find God only along the way. God "appears at the crossroads," Francis told Brazil's bishops on July 27, 2013. We find God and simultaneously seek God in what is new. There occurs an interplay between being near and not yet near. This process engages us whether we are believers or not. God encounters us, but we do not recognize him—as happened to the disappointed disciples on the road to Emmaus (Luke 24:13–35). Viewed in this manner, the Creed—as the great councils of the early church formulated it—is no longer a barrier between those who believe and those who don't. Rather, it unites all of us.

This book is an introduction to a spiritual way through the Apostles' Creed. Francis, who, along with every Jesuit, has walked through the Spiritual Exercises of Saint Ignatius of Loyola, is our retreat director. The texts in this book, which I have gathered from his statements and writings, have differing literary genres, from pastoral letters to snippets from his talks. As a rule, they originated after his election to the papacy on March 13, 2013. Sometimes, above all in the first chapter, I have also selected earlier texts because they seem to me to be especially powerful.

I hope that readers will not be confused by the diversity of literary genres and the pope's unique formulations. Please approach these texts as an opportunity to reflect on our ancient Creed through new lenses.

The expression "to reflect on" functions here in its two senses. These texts by Francis are not meant to be studied or academically investigated, but to be reflected on.

Most inspirational for me are the selections from Pope Francis's sermons at his daily early morning Masses in the Casa Santa Marta, the Vatican's guest house in which he resides. Here, the "pastor of Santa Marta" speaks every time with complete freedom. Thus, with these statements, we come closest to his way of thinking and speaking.

All selections from papal texts in this book are available in the official versions, with the exception of the sermons at Santa Marta, for which there are no official versions of the complete texts. (In this book the selections from the sermons are derived from the summaries that appear in *l'Osservatore Romano,* which combine quotations and paraphrases of his remarks.)

The introduction to each chapter coincides with the pertinent section of the Apostles' Creed. The book's appendix contains some selections from the pope's first encyclical on the Christian faith, *Lumen Fidei*. I wish all readers a "*Buen camino!*" which is the centuries-old greeting of pilgrims on the Camino of Santiago de Compostela. This greeting appears to me to be very apt in connection with this book. Therefore: "*Buen camino!*"—"Good journey!"

—Translated by Robert A. Krieg

The Apostles' Creed

I believe in God,
the Father Almighty,
Creator of heaven and earth,
and in Jesus Christ, his only Son, our Lord,
who was conceived by the Holy Spirit,
born of the Virgin Mary,
suffered under Pontius Pilate,
was crucified, died and was buried;
he descended into hell;
on the third day he rose again from the dead;
he ascended into heaven,
and is seated at the right hand of God
the Father Almighty;
from there he will come to judge the living and the dead.
I believe in the Holy Spirit,
the holy catholic Church,
the communion of saints,
the forgiveness of sins,
the resurrection of the body,
and life everlasting.
Amen.

✠

I Believe

WITH MY LIFE

Shortly before his ordination to the priesthood on December 13, 1969, Jorge Mario Bergoglio, the current pope, composed "in a moment of spiritual intensity" his own confession of faith, which he preserved over the decades. It gives witness to a very direct translation of "I believe" into his own life. This testimony expresses his understanding that the Christian faith should belong to one's actual life. A few years earlier, Pope Paul VI had formulated a Credo at the conclusion of the Second Vatican Council which relies much more closely on the original text of the Apostles' Creed.

Pope Francis speaks early in his creed of other people. He believes, he writes, in the goodness of people, using a figure of speech that strikingly recalls the similarly fashioned words of Anne Frank in her diary, written under very different circumstances.

The personal associations in Francis's creed are numerous. Bergoglios's reference to an early spring day concerns the Rite of Reconciliation (confession) in which he participated with Father Duarte in Buenos Aires on September 21, 1953, and which marked the beginning of his vocation to the priesthood. (In Argentina, as in the entire southern hemisphere, September 21st is the first day of spring.)

I want to believe in God the Father who loves me like a child, and in Jesus the Lord who infused my life with His Spirit, to make me smile and so carry me to the eternal kingdom of life.

I believe in the Church.

I believe in my life story, which was pierced by God's loving gaze, who on that spring day of September 21st came out to meet me to invite me to follow him.

I believe in my pain, made fruitless by the egotism in which I take refuge.

I believe in the stinginess of my soul, which seeks to take without giving.

I believe in the goodness of others, and that I must love them without fear and without betraying them, never seeking my own security.

I believe in the religious life.

I believe I wish to love a lot.

I believe in the burning death of each day, from which I flee but which smiles at me, inviting me to accept her.

I believe in God's patience, as good and as welcoming as a summer's night.

I believe that Dad is with the Lord in heaven.

I believe that Fr. Duarte is there, too, interceding for my priesthood.

I believe in Mary, my Mother, who loves me and will never leave me...

And I believe in the surprise of each day, in which will be manifest love, strength, betrayal, and sin, which will be always with me until that definitive encounter with that marvelous face which I do not know, which always escapes me, but which I wish to know and love. Amen.

—*Quoted in Austen Ivereigh,* The Great Reformer *(New York: Picador, 2015)*

For further reflection: What would be my own confession of faith? What do I promise myself from the Creed?

In What Is Handed On

Without faith one cannot live without sinning and always forgiving. We truly need the light of faith, that faith which we have received, the faith of a merciful Father, of a Son who gave his life for us, of a Spirit who is inside us and helps us grow, the faith in the Church, the faith in the baptized and holy people of God. And this is a gift: faith is a gift. No one receives faith from books or by going to conferences. After all, precisely because faith is a gift of God who comes to us, the apostles said to Jesus: "Increase our faith!"

—*Morning Homily, November 10, 2014*

Everyone who abides in God, everyone who has been born of God, everyone who abides in love conquers the world. And that victory is our faith... It's powerful! Because the victory that has conquered the world is our faith. Our faith can do anything; it's victorious! This is a truth that it would be lovely to tell ourselves often, because so often we're defeated Christians, who don't believe faith is a victory, who don't live by this faith. And if we don't live by this faith we're defeated. The world conquers, the prince of this world...

This faith asks two things of us: to confess and to trust. First of all, faith is confessing God—but the God who revealed himself to us from the time of our fathers up till now, the God of history. That's what we declare every day in the Creed. But it's one thing to say the Creed from our heart and another to parrot it: "I believe in God, I believe in Jesus Christ, I believe..." Do I believe in what I say? Is this confession of faith true or do I say it from memory because it has to be said? Or do I only half believe?

So we must confess the faith. And confess it all, not just part of it! But we must also keep it all as it has been handed down to us by tradition. The whole faith! How can we know if we confess the faith properly? Here is the sign: anyone who confesses the faith properly, the whole faith, is capable of worshiping God. It's a sign that may seem a bit strange, because we know how to ask God for things, how to thank God. But worshiping God, praising God, is something more. Only someone who has this strong faith is able to worship.

In worshiping, I dare say that the temperature of the Church is a bit low: we Christians don't have a great capacity for worship (although some do) because in our confession of faith we aren't convinced. Or we're [only] half convinced . . .

The man or woman who has faith trusts in God. He or she trusts. At a dark moment in his life Paul said: "I know the one in whom I have trusted. God. The Lord Jesus." And trust leads us to hope. Just as the confession of faith leads us to worship and praise God, trusting in God leads us to an attitude of hope.

But there are so many Christians with a watered-down hope, a watered-down hope that isn't strong. And what's the reason for his weak hope? Of course it's lack of the strength and courage to trust in the Lord. But to be victorious Christians, we must believe, confessing the faith and also keeping the faith, and trusting in God, the Lord. That's the victory that has conquered the world: our faith.

—Morning Homily, January 9, 2014

For further reflection: How do I say the Apostles' Creed? Do I repeat it mindlessly? A suggestion: Say the Creed once in its entirety and reflect on it.

Walking. This verb makes us reflect on the course of history, that long journey which is the history of salvation, starting with Abraham, our father in faith, whom the Lord called one day to set out, to go forth from his country toward the land which he would show him. From that time on, our identity as believers has been that of a people making its pilgrim way toward the promised land. This history has always been accompanied by the Lord! He is ever faithful to his covenant and to his promises. Because he is faithful, "God is light, and in him there is no darkness at all" (1 Jn 1:5). Yet on the part of the people there are times of both light and darkness, fidelity and infidelity, obedience and rebellion; times of being a pilgrim people and times of being a people adrift.

In our personal history too, there are both bright and dark moments, lights and shadows. If we love God and our brothers and sisters, we walk in the light; but if our heart is closed, if we are dominated by pride, deceit, self-seeking, then darkness falls within us and around us. "Whoever hates his brother," writes the apostle John, "is in the darkness; he walks in the darkness, and does not know the way to go, because the darkness has blinded his eyes" (1 Jn 2:11). A people who walk, but as a pilgrim people who do not want to go astray.

—Sermon for Midnight Mass, December 24, 2013

In a Door that Opens

In his apostolic letter Porta Fidei ("Door of Faith," October 2011), Pope Benedict XVI called for a "Year of Faith" during 2012–2013. The occasion was the fiftieth anniversary of the conclusion of the Second Vatican Council (1962–1965). In a pastoral letter in 2012, Jorge Mario Bergoglio as the archbishop of Buenos Aires, employed the image of faith as a door. At the end of February 2013 Benedict stepped aside. On March 13, 2013, Archbishop Bergoglio was elected to the papacy and assumed leadership of the Year of Faith. The archbishop's 2012 pastoral letter characteristically conveys his conviction that the Christian faith is not a "private matter": "In order to confess the faith in words, we must live it in our hearts and show it in our actions."

Dear Brothers and Sisters:

Among the most striking experiences of the last decades is finding doors closed. Little by little increasing insecurity has made us bolt doors, employ means of vigilance, install security cameras, and mistrust strangers who call at our door.

Nonetheless, in some places there are doors that are still open. The closed door is really a symbol of our today. It is something more than a simple sociological fact; it is an existential reality that is imposing itself as a way of life, a way of confronting reality, others, and the future. The bolted door of my house, the place of my intimate life, my dreams, hopes, sufferings, and moments of happiness, is locked against others. And it is not simply a matter of the physical house; it is also the whole area of my life, of my heart. All the time there are fewer who can cross that threshold. The security of reinforced doors protects the insecurity of a life that is becoming more fragile and less open to the riches of the life and the love of others.

The image of an open door has always been a symbol of light, friendship, happiness, liberty, and trust. How we need to recover them. The closed door does us harm, reduces and separates us.

We begin the Year of Faith and, paradoxically, the image that the pope proposes is that of a door, a door through which we must pass to be able to find what we need so much. The Church, through the voice and heart of its pastor, Benedict XVI, invites us to cross the threshold, to take an interior and free step: to animate ourselves to enter a new life.

The phrase "door to faith" brings us back to the Acts of the Apostles: "On arriving, they gathered the Church together and told them what God had done through them and how he had opened the door of faith to the Gentiles" (Acts 14:27). God always takes the initiative and he does not want anyone to be excluded. God calls at the door of our hearts: Look, I am at the door, calling: if anyone hears my voice and opens the door, I shall enter his house and dine with him and him with me (Rev 3:20). Faith is a grace, a gift of God . . .

Crossing through that door presupposes the beginning of a way or journey that lasts a lifetime, as we pass in front of so many doors open to us today, many of them false doors, doors that invite us in a very attractive but lying manner to go down a road that promises an empty narcissistic happiness that has an expiration date; doors that lead to crossroads where, no matter which option we follow, will lead, sooner or later, to suffering and confusion; doors that lead nowhere and have no guarantees for the future.

While the doors of houses are closed, the doors of shopping malls are always open. One passes through the door of faith, one crosses that threshold, when the Word of God is announced and the heart allows itself to be shaped by that grace which transforms, a grace which has a concrete name, and that name is Jesus. Jesus is the door (Jn 10:9). He, and only He, is and will always be the door. No one goes to the Father except through him (Jn 14:6). If there is no Christ, there is no way to God. As the door, he opens the way to God, and as Good Shepherd, he is the only one who looks after us at the price of his own life.

Jesus is the door and he knocks on our door so that we may allow him to cross the threshold of our lives. "Don't be afraid, open the doors wide for Christ," Blessed John Paul II told us at the beginning of his papacy: to open the doors of our hearts as the disciples of Emmaus did, asking him to stay with us so that we might pass through the doors of faith, so that the Lord himself might bring us to understand the reasons why we believe and that we may then go out and tell others. Faith presumes that we decide to be with the Lord, to live with him and share him with our brothers and sisters.

We give thanks to God for this opportunity to realize the value of our lives as children of God through this journey of faith which began for us with the waters of baptism, that never-ending and life-giving dew which makes us children of God and brothers and sisters in the Church. The purpose, the objective [of this Year of Faith] is that we meet with God with whom we have already entered into communion and who wishes to restore us, purify us, raise us up and sanctify us, and give us the happiness that our hearts crave.

—Cardinal Bergoglio's October 2012 Pastoral Letter for the Year of Faith

To begin this Year of Faith is [to answer] a new call to deepen in our lives this faith that we have received. Professing the faith with our lips implies living it in our hearts and showing it in our works: a witness and a public commitment. The disciple of Christ, son or daughter of the Church, can never think that believing is a private act... Considering our reality as missionary disciples, we ask, "What does crossing the threshold of faith challenge us to do?"

Crossing the threshold of faith challenges us to discover that although it seems today that death reigns in its various forms and that history is ruled by the law of the most powerful or the most cunning, and although hatred and ambition operate as driving forces of so many human struggles, nevertheless we are absolutely and decisively convinced that this sad reality can change and must change, because "if God is for us, who can be against us?" (Rom 8:31, 37).

Crossing the threshold of faith means not being ashamed to have the heart of a child who, because he still believes in impossible things, can live in hope—the one thing that is capable of giving meaning and transforming history. It is to ask without ceasing, to pray without faltering, and to adore so as be transfigured by what we contemplate.

Crossing the threshold of faith leads us to beseech for each one of us the "mind . . . which was in Jesus Christ" (Phil 2:5), so that we may experience a new way of thinking, of communicating, of being in the family, of planning for the future, of living out the virtue of charity and our vocation.

Crossing the threshold of faith is acting with trust in the power of the Holy Spirit who is present in the Church and who also manifests himself in the signs of the times; it is accompanying the constant movement of life and of history without falling into the paralyzing defeatism that regards any time in the past as being better; it is a sense of urgency about thinking in a new way, contributing in a new way, creating in a new way, kneading into life "the new leaven of justice and holiness" (cf. 1 Cor 5:8).

Crossing the threshold of faith implies keeping our sense of wonder, having a heart that has not lazily settled into routine, but is capable of recognizing that every time a woman brings a child into this world she is betting on life and on the future, that when we protect the innocence of children we guarantee the truth of a tomorrow, and when we act as caregivers for an elderly person we perform an act of justice and cherish our roots.

Crossing the threshold of faith is work performed with dignity as a response to a call to service, with the self-sacrifice of one who gets up day after day to begin again without slackening, as though all that had already been done were just one step in the journey toward the Kingdom, toward fullness of life. It is the silent hope after the daily sowing, contemplating the fruit gathered, thanking the Lord because he is good, and asking him not to abandon the work of his hands (Ps 138).

Crossing the threshold of faith demands striving for freedom and peaceful coexistence—even though everyone around us wavers—in the certainty that the Lord is asking us to do justice, to love kindness, and to walk humbly with our God (Micah 6:8).

Crossing the threshold of faith entails the ongoing conversion of our attitudes, the habits and the customs by which we live; voicing our thoughts in new, unvarnished terms, without papering over differences; giving new form to everything and everyone imprinted by Jesus Christ, touched by his hand and his gospel of life; encouraging one another to do something unprecedented for society and for the Church; because "if anyone is in Christ, he is a new creation" (2 Cor 5:17–21).

Crossing the threshold of faith enables us to forgive and to be able to smile. It leads us to draw near to everyone who lives a marginalized existence and call him or her by name; to care for the frailties of those who are weakest and to support their tottering steps, certain that whatever we do for the least of our brethren we do for Jesus himself (Mt 25:40).

Crossing the threshold of faith means celebrating life, allowing ourselves to be transformed so that we become one with Jesus at the table of the Eucharist celebrated in community, and from there occupying our hands and our hearts with the great project of the Kingdom: all the rest will be given us as well (Mt 6:33).

Crossing the threshold of faith is living in the spirit of the [Second Vatican] Council and of Aparecida [Brazil, site of the Fifth General Conference of Latin American Bishops in 2007], in the Church of the open doors, not only so that we may receive the gospel but so that we may go out and fill with the gospel message the streets and the lives of the people of our times.

Crossing the threshold of faith for our archdiocesan church means to feel that we are confirmed in our mission to be a church that lives, prays, and works in a missionary key.

Crossing the threshold of faith is, finally, accepting the newness of the life of the Risen Lord in our poor flesh so as to make it a sign of his new life.

Meditating on all these things, we look to Mary, that she, the Virgin Mother, might accompany us in this crossing of the threshold of faith and draw down upon our church in Buenos Aires the Holy Spirit, so that, as in Nazareth, we might—just like her—adore the Lord and go out to proclaim the marvels that he has done among us.

—Cardinal Bergoglio's October 2012 Pastoral Letter for the Year of Faith

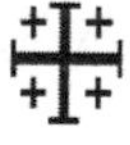

For further reflection: Is my door open or closed? How would I complete this sentence: For me the threshold of faith means...

In Conversations with Non-Christians

When I speak with atheists, I will sometimes discuss social concerns, but I do not propose the problem of God as a starting point, except in the case that they propose it to me. If this occurs, I tell them why I believe. But that which is human is so rich to share and to work at that very easily we can mutually complement our richness. As I am a believer, I know that these riches are a gift from God. I also know that the other person, the atheist, does not know that. I do not approach the relationship in order to proselytize or convert the atheist; I respect him and I show myself as I am. Where there is knowledge, there begins to appear esteem, affection, and friendship. I do not have any type of reluctance, nor would I say that his life is condemned, because I am convinced that I do not have the right to make a judgment about the honesty of that person; even less, if he shows me those human virtues that exalt others and do me good.

—Jorge Mario Bergoglio in conversation with Rabbi Abraham Skorka,
On Heaven and Earth *(New York: Image, 2013), 12*

The spiritual experience of encounter with God is not controllable. One feels that God is there, one has the certainty, but he cannot control God. We are made to subdue nature; that is what God commands. We cannot, however, subdue our Creator. As a result, in the experience of God there is always an unanswered question, an opportunity to be submerged in faith . . . We can say what God is not, we can speak of his attributes, but we cannot say what he is.

—Jorge Mario Bergoglio in conversation with Rabbi Abraham Skorka,
On Heaven and Earth *(New York: Image, 2013), 14*

In the late summer of 2013, shortly after Bergoglios's election to the papacy, the Italian publicist and agnostic Eugenio Scalfari published in the daily newspaper La Repubblica *an open letter with numerous questions for the pope. The pope's response, excerpts of which are reprinted below, was subsequently published in* La Repubblica.

I believe that in the first [of your] two questions, what interests you is to understand the attitude of the Church toward those who do not share faith in Jesus. Above all, you ask if the God of Christians forgives those who do not believe and who do not seek faith. Given the premise, and this is fundamental, that the mercy of God is limitless for those who turn to him with a sincere and contrite heart, the issue for the unbeliever lies in obeying his or her conscience. There is sin, even for those who have no faith, when conscience is not followed. Listening to and obeying conscience means deciding in the face of what is understood to be good or evil. It is on the basis of this choice that the goodness or evil of our actions is determined.

Secondly, you ask me whether it is erroneous or a sin to follow the line of thought which holds that there is no absolute, and therefore no absolute truth, but only a series of relative and subjective truths. To begin with, I would not speak about "absolute" truths, even for believers, in the sense that [what is] absolute is that which is disconnected and bereft of all relationship. Truth, according to the Christian faith, is the love of God for us in Jesus Christ.

Therefore, truth is a relationship. As such each one of us receives the truth and expresses it from within, that is to say, according to one's own circumstances, culture, and situation in life, etc. This does not mean that truth is variable and subjective, quite the contrary. But it does signify that it comes to us always and only as a way and a life. Did not Jesus himself say: "I am the way, the truth, and the life?" In other words, truth, being completely one with love, demands humility and an openness to be sought, received, and expressed. Therefore, we must have a correct understanding of the terms and, perhaps, in order to overcome being bogged down by conflicting absolute positions, we need to redefine the issues in depth. I believe this is absolutely necessary...

In your final question, you ask me:...when man disappears from the earth, will the capacity to contemplate God disappear? Undoubtedly, the greatness of the human person resides in the ability to reflect on God, that is to say, to be able to live in a conscious and responsible relationship with him. But this relationship is between two realities. God—and this is my thinking and experience, shared by many from past and present!—is not an idea, even if a lofty one [or] the fruit of human thought; God is a reality with a capital "R." Jesus reveals to us that this reality is a Father of infinite goodness and mercy, in relation with whom he lives. Furthermore, when earthly human existence ends—and for the Christian faith, at any rate, this world as we know it is destined to pass—men and women will not cease to exist and, in a way that we do not understand, this is also true of the universe created with them. Scripture speaks of a "new heaven and a new earth" and states that at the end God will be "all in all" in a time and in a manner that lie beyond us, but toward which we progress in faith with expectation and desire.

Dear Dr. Scalfari, I conclude my reflections, which are a response to your thoughts and questions. Please receive them as a preliminary reply, but one which is sincere and full of hope, along with the invitation to walk this path together. The Church, despite all of the sluggishness, infidelities, errors, and sins that are committed and are still being committed by her members, has no other meaning or purpose than to live and witness to Jesus: he who has been sent by Abba, "to preach good news to the poor, to proclaim release to the captives and recovery of sight to the blind, to set at liberty those who are oppressed, to proclaim the acceptable year of the Lord" (Lk 4:18–19).

With fraternal good wishes,
Francis

—Letter to a Nonbeliever, Eugenio Scalfari, September 11, 2013

For further reflection: "Truth is a relationship." This is a surprising statement, or is it? How do I understand it? And, does it have consequences for my creed? In a sermon at a morning Mass, the pope once said, "Truth is an encounter." Have I had such an encounter?

Early in the year 2014, the pope was interviewed by youth from Belgium. During the session, one young woman said to him, "I do not believe in God. However, your actions and your ideals are inspiring to me. Do you perhaps have a message for all of us, for young Christians and also for people who do not believe or have a different faith or believe in a different manner?"

I believe we must look, in our way of speaking, for authenticity. And for me, authenticity is this: I am speaking with brothers. We are all brothers. Believers, non-believers, of this or that religious confession, Jews, Muslims . . . we are all brothers. Man is at the center of history, and this is very important for me: man is at the center. In this moment of history, man has been removed from the center, he has slid to the fringe, and at the center—at least at this moment—is power, money. And we must work for persons, for man and woman, who are the image of God.

—Interview with young people from Flanders, Beligium, at the Vatican, March 31, 2014

During this interview, another young woman asked how someone could give the best witness to the Christian faith. The pope answered:

Witness with simplicity, because if you go with your faith like a flag, like the Crusades, and you engage in proselytism, that's no good. The best way is witness, but humble witness: "I am like this," with humility, without triumphalism. That's another sin of ours, another bad attitude, triumphalism. Jesus wasn't triumphalist, and history also teaches us not to be triumphalist, because the great triumphalists were defeated. Witness: this is a key, it interpolates. I give it with humility, without engaging in proselytism. I offer it, it is so. And this does not create fear, does not go on a Crusade.

—Interview with young people from Flanders, Beligium, at the Vatican, March 31, 2014

And Which Have Consequences

Jesus condemns people with good manners but bad habits, because it is one thing to appear good and beautiful, but inner truth is another thing. In the same way, it isn't good to be bound exclusively to the letter of the law, because law alone doesn't save. Law saves when it leads you to the source of salvation.

Jesus condemned cosmetic spirituality. This refers to the [spirituality of] people who like to take walks in the town square, and to be seen while they pray, and to wear a dismal face while they fast...

Faith is not only reciting the Creed: we all believe in the Father, in the Son, and in the Holy Spirit, in life everlasting...But if our faith is immobile and inactive, then it's of no use. Thus, what is important in Jesus Christ is the faith that becomes active in charity...

Today it will [be] good to think about my faith, my Christian life: Is it a Christian life of cosmetics, of appearance? Or is it a Christian life with a faith that is active in charity? Everyone can examine his or her conscience before God. And it is good for us to do so.

—Morning Homily, October 14, 2014

Faith is never abstract: it must be a witness. The apostle James gives this teaching, which is an exhortation about faith... What James is saying is clear: faith that doesn't bear fruit in works isn't faith. We too often make a mistake about this. We hear someone saying: "I have so much faith!" or "I believe everything!" but perhaps the person saying this lives a lukewarm, feeble life. So their faith is just a theory, not a living force in their life.

When the apostle James speaks about faith, he's talking about doctrine, the content of faith. And it's as if he were saying to each one of us: "But you can know all the commandments, all the prophecies, all the truths of faith, but if all that isn't translated into practice, into works, it's no good."

Theoretically we can even recite the Creed without faith. There are so many people who do that! Even the demons! Actually, the demons know very well what is said in the Creed and know that it's true. "They shudder," says the apostle James, "because they know it's true," even though they don't have faith. Demons know all theology, they know Denzinger [the classic manual of doctrinal formulations] by heart, but they don't have faith. For having faith doesn't mean having knowledge: having faith means accepting God's message brought to us by Jesus Christ, living by it and carrying it out.

There are signs by which to recognize someone who knows what we're supposed to believe but who doesn't have faith. The first sign showing knowledge of theology without faith is casuistry [the use of clever but unsound reasoning, particularly in relation to moral issues]. There were those who went to Jesus with casuistical questions, such as: "Is it lawful to pay taxes to Caesar?" Casuistry is used by people who think they have faith, but know only the content of faith. So when we find Christians who merely ask whether it's lawful to do this or whether the Church could do that, it means that either they don't have faith or it's too weak.

The second sign is ideology. There are Christians who think of the faith as a system of ideas, an ideology. That's a risk that was also present in Jesus' time. The apostle James says of these ideologists of the faith that they're the Antichrist. So, those who fall into casuistry or ideology are Christians who know the doctrine but lack faith. Like the demons. With the difference that the demons shudder, but these people don't: they live peacefully…

The gospels describe two contrasting attitudes: on the one hand there are those who have doctrine and know things, and on the other there are those who have faith. Between them there is one certainty: Faith always leads to witness. Faith is a meeting with Jesus Christ, with God.

That meeting leads to bearing witness, as the apostle James stresses in his letter. He says that faith without works, faith that doesn't involve you, that doesn't lead you to bear witness, isn't faith. It's just words. Nothing but words.

—Morning Homily, February 21, 2014

Faith is first of all a gift we have received. But in order to bear fruit, God's grace always demands our openness to him, our free and tangible response. Christ comes to bring us the mercy of a God who saves. We are asked to trust in him, to respond to the gift of his love with a good life made up of actions motivated by faith and love.

—General Audience, April 24, 2013

What Christ did in us was a re-creation. Christ's blood has re-created us; it's a second creation. And if, before, our whole life, our whole body, our whole soul, all our habits were on the road of sin, of iniquity, then after this re-creation we must make the effort to walk in the way of uprightness, of sanctification. Paul uses this word: holiness. We have all been baptized. At that time we were babies, and our parents declared the act of faith in our name: I believe in Jesus Christ who has forgiven our sins.

We have to take up this faith again and carry it forward in the way we live. Living as a Christian means carrying on this faith in Christ, this re-creation, carrying on the works that arise from that faith. The important thing is faith, but works are the fruit of this faith: carrying on these works for sanctification. So, the first sanctification—which was Christ's work—the first sanctification that we received in baptism, must grow, it must advance.

If you become accustomed to a so-so life and say, "I believe in Jesus Christ, but I'll live as I please," then that does not sanctify you, it won't do, it's nonsense. But if you say, "Yes, I'm a sinner, I'm weak," and you always go to the Lord and say, "Lord, you've got the strength, give me faith; you can heal me," through the sacrament of reconciliation, then even our imperfections can become part of this way of sanctification.

First, the act of faith. Before we were accepted by Jesus Christ who re-created us with his blood, we were on the way of unrighteousness; afterwards, we are on the way of sanctification, but we have to take it seriously. That means doing works of uprightness. Above all, worship God, and then do what Jesus advises us: help one another, give food to the hungry, give drink to the thirsty, visit the sick, visit prisoners. These works are works that Jesus did during his lifetime, works of uprightness, works of re-creation. When we give the hungry something to eat, we re-create hope in them and so it is with the other works. But if we don't accept the faith and don't live by it, our Christianity is just a memory: yes, I was baptized, that's the faith of my baptism, but I live as I choose.

Without an awareness of before and after, our Christianity's no good to anyone. So it becomes hypocrisy:

I say I am a Christian but I live as a pagan. Sometimes we call this being halfway Christians, people who don't seriously consider that they have been sanctified by Christ's blood. And if we don't take that sanctification seriously we become lukewarm Christians: yes, yes, no, no... A bit like what our mothers called watered down Christians: so-so Christians, with a coating of Christianity, a coating of catechism, but inside there isn't real conversion, there isn't that burning conviction St. Paul had: "I have suffered the loss of all things, and regard them as rubbish, in order that I may gain Christ and be found in him."

That should be a Christian's passion: to let go of everything that distances us from Christ the Lord; to let go of everything that distances us from the act of faith in him, the act of faith in our re-creation through his blood. In Christ all things are made new. Everything is new...

Perhaps the question we should ask ourselves today is: "Do I want to take my Christianity seriously? Do I believe that I've been re-crated by Christ's blood and do I want to carry on this re-creation to the day in which the new Jerusalem, the new creation will appear? Or am I a halfway Christian?'"

—Morning Homily, October 24, 2013

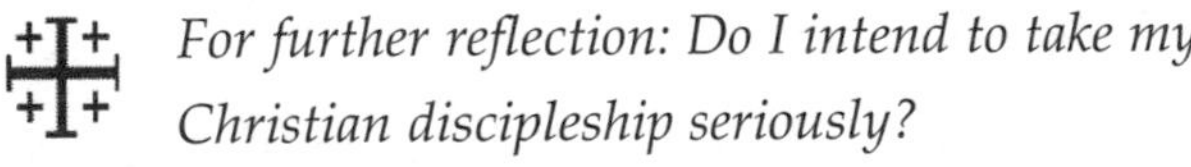

For further reflection: Do I intend to take my Christian discipleship seriously?

Dear brothers, the profession of faith we are now renewing together is not a formal act. Rather, it means renewing our response to the "Follow me" with which John's gospel ends (21:19). It leads to living our life in accordance with God's plan, committing our whole self to the Lord Jesus. The discernment that knows and takes on the thoughts, expectations and needs of the people of our time stems from this.

—*Address at the Celebration of the Creed with the Italian Bishops, May 23, 2013*

✠

I Believe in God

Jesus is our true friend. It is he who accompanies us and teaches us to pray. And our prayer must thus be Trinitarian.

Often one hears the question, "Do you believe?" "Yes, yes!" "What do you believe in?" "In God!" "But what is God for you?" "God is God!"

God exists—but don't be shocked now! God does not exist as a solitary, abstract idea. The Father, the Son, and the Holy Spirit exist: these are Persons, and not an abstract idea in the air. This "Mist God" does not exist! There are only Persons.

Jesus is the companion on the journey who gives us what we ask; the Father who cares for us and loves us; and the Holy Spirit, who is the gift, is that "more" that the Father gives, for which our conscience does not dare to hope.

—*Morning Homily, October 9, 2014*

For further reflection: "God does not exist. A solitary God does not exist . . ." Does this statement shock me? How concrete is my image of God?

There is a temptation to seek God in the past or in a possible future. God is certainly in the past because we can see the footprints. And God is also in the future as a promise. But the "concrete" God, so to speak, is today. For this reason, complaining never helps us find God. The complaints of today about how "barbaric" the world is—these complaints sometimes end up giving birth within the Church to desires to establish order in the sense of pure conservation, as a defense. No: God is to be encountered in the world of today.

God manifests himself in historical revelation, in history. Time initiates processes, and space crystallizes them. God is in history, in the processes.

We must not focus on occupying the spaces where power is exercised, but rather on starting long-run historical processes. We must initiate processes rather than occupy spaces. God manifests himself in time and is present in the processes of history. This gives priority to actions that give birth to new historical dynamics. And it requires patience, waiting.

Finding God in all things is not an "empirical *eureka*." When we desire to encounter God, we would like to verify him immediately by an empirical method. But you cannot meet God this way. God is found in the gentle breeze perceived by Elijah. The senses that find God are the ones Saint Ignatius called spiritual senses. Ignatius asks us to open our spiritual sensitivity to encounter God beyond a purely empirical approach. A contemplative attitude is necessary: it is the feeling that you are moving along the good path of understanding and affection toward things and situations. Profound peace, spiritual consolation, love of God and love of all things in God—this is the sign that you are on this right path.

—"A Big Heart Open to God," interview in America, *September 30, 2013*

The book of Job is a continuous discussion about the definition of God. There are four wise men who elaborate this theological search and everything ends with Job's expression: "By hearsay I had heard of you, but now my eye has seen you." Job's final image of God is different from his vision of God in the beginning. The intention of this story is that the notion that the four theologians have is not true, because God always is being sought and found. We are presented with this paradox: we seek him to find him and because we find him, we seek him.

—Jorge Mario Bergoglio in conversation with Rabbi Abraham Skorka,
On Heaven and Earth *(New York: Image, 2013), 15*

. . . The Father

One of the pope's favorite biblical texts is Jesus' parable of the prodigal son in Luke's gospel (15:11–32). Francis has highlighted in this parable "that the father already sees the son coming from afar because he was waiting for him and every day went out to the terrace in order to see whether the son had come back" (Sermon at Mass on March 28, 2014). This means that the father awaits the return of his son and keeps watch for him. In Pope Francis's words, God, the Father, is "the God who always awaits us."

If you want to know a father's tenderness, try turning to God: try and then tell me! However many sins we may have committed, God always awaits us and is ready to welcome us and to give us a homecoming party. He's a father who never tires of forgiving and doesn't check whether the final "balance" is negative: God can do nothing but love . . .

God never tires. We see him over many centuries, with so many apostasies of his people. Yet he always returns, because our God is a God who awaits us. Even Adam left paradise with a punishment and a promise. The Lord is faithful to his promise because he cannot deny himself: he is faithful!

So God has awaited all of us, throughout history. Indeed he is a God who always awaits us. Contemplate that beautiful image of the father and the prodigal son. Luke's gospel tells us that the father sees his son in the distance because he is looking out to see whether his son will come back. So the father is awaiting his son's return and when he sees him coming he rushes out and puts his arms round him. Perhaps on the way the son had prepared what he would say when he got home: "Father, I have sinned against heaven and before you. I am no longer worthy to be called your son." But his father didn't let him speak; he embraced his son and covered his mouth with a kiss.

Jesus' parable makes us understand who our father is: God who always awaits us. Someone might say: "But, Father, I have so many sins that I don't know whether he'll be happy with me!" Give it a try! If you want to know this Father's tenderness, go to him and give it a try! Then come and tell me! Because the God who awaits us is also the God who forgives: it's we who grow tired of asking for forgiveness. But he never tires: seventy times seven! Always! On with forgiveness!

Of course, from a business viewpoint the balance is negative, that's true! He always loses, he loses out on the balance. But he wins in love because he—we can say this—is the first one to fulfill the commandment of love: he loves, he can't do anything else . . .

Each person's life, each man's, each woman's who has the courage to approach the Lord will encounter the joy of God's banquet. May this word help us to think about our

Father, the Father who always awaits us, who always forgives us, and who gives a party when we come home!

—*Morning Homily, March 28, 2014*

Every good father needs his child: he waits for the child, loves, forgives, wants his child near himself, as close as a hen wants her chicks... Recall how King David wept over his son: "O my son Absalom, my son, my son Absalom. Would that I had died instead of you. O Absalom, my son, my son!"

This is the heart of a father, who never rejects his son. It makes us think of the first thing we say about God in the Creed: "I believe in God the Father." It makes us think of God's fatherhood. That's how God is with us. But someone might object: "But Father, God doesn't cry!" Of course he does! Remember when Jesus wept over Jerusalem? "Jerusalem, Jerusalem, how often have I wanted to gather your children as a hen gathers her chicks under her wings!" So God weeps; Jesus wept for us. And that weeping is the cry of a father who wants us all with him at difficult times.

Today we can meditate on these two images: David weeping and the leader of the synagogue throwing himself at Jesus' feet without shame or fear of looking ridiculous, because their children were at risk. Let us renew our profession of faith, saying "I believe in God the Father" and ask the Holy Spirit to teach us to say "Abba, Father." Because, it is a grace to be able to say "Father" to God with our whole heart.

—*Morning Homily, February 4, 2014*

God's steadfast love for his people is manifest and wholly fulfilled in Jesus Christ, who, in order to honor God's bond with his people, made himself our slave, stripped himself of his glory, and assumed the form of a servant. Out of love he did not surrender to our ingratitude, not even in the face of rejection. Saint Paul reminds us: "If we are faithless, he, Jesus, remains faithful, for he cannot deny himself" (2 Tim 2:13). Jesus remains faithful, he never betrays us: even when we are wrong, he always waits for us to forgive us: he is the face of the merciful Father.

This love, this steadfastness of the Lord manifests the humility of his heart: Jesus did not come to conquer men like the kings and the powerful of this world, but he came to offer love with gentleness and humility. This is how he defined himself: "Learn from me; for I am gentle and lowly in heart" (Mt 11:29). And the significance of the Feast of the Sacred Heart of Jesus . . . is to discover ever more and to let ourselves be enfolded by the humble faithfulness and the gentleness of Christ's love, revelation of the Father's mercy. We can experience and savor the tenderness of this love at every stage of life: in times of joy and of sadness, in times of good health and of frailty and . . . sickness.

God's faithfulness teaches us to accept life as a circumstance of his love and he allows us to witness this love to our brothers and sisters in humble and gentle service ...Dear brothers and sisters, in Christ we contemplate God's faithfulness. Every act, every word of Jesus reveals the merciful and steadfast love of the Father. And so before him we ask ourselves: How is my love for my neighbor? Do I know how to be faithful? Or am I inconsistent, following my moods and impulses? Each of us can answer in our own mind. But above all we can say to the Lord: Lord Jesus, render my heart ever more like yours, full of love and faithfulness.

—*Homily at the Gemelli Hospital in Rome, June 27, 2014*

The origin of the darkness which envelops the world is lost in the night of the ages. Let us think back to that dark moment when the first crime of humanity was committed, when the hand of Cain, blinded by envy, killed his brother Abel (cf. Gen 4:8). As a result, the unfolding of the centuries has been marked by violence, wars, hatred, and oppression. But God, who placed a sense of expectation within man made in his image and likeness, was waiting. God was waiting. He waited for so long that perhaps at a certain point it seemed he should have given up. But he could not give up because he could not deny himself (cf. 2 Tim 2:13). Therefore he continued to wait patiently in the face of the corruption of man and peoples. The patience of God. How difficult it is to comprehend this: God's patience toward us.

Through the course of history, the light that shatters the darkness reveals to us that God is Father and that his patient fidelity is stronger than darkness and corruption...God does not know outbursts of anger or impatience; he is always there, like the father in the parable of the prodigal son, waiting to catch from afar a glimpse of the lost son as he returns; and every day, with patience. The patience of God.

—Homily for Midnight Mass, December 24, 2014

In accepting the gift of faith, believers become a new creation; they receive a new being; as God's children, they are now "sons in the Son." The phrase "Abba, Father," so characteristic of Jesus' own experience, now becomes the core of the Christian experience (cf. Rom 8:15). The life of faith, as a filial existence, is the acknowledgment of a primordial and radical gift which upholds our lives.

Encyclical Lumen Fidei, *19*

...The Almighty

Francis hardly speaks at all about the Almighty God, but he often speaks about God's predilection for the small, the least. In his Jesuit-trained spirituality, God's greatness is manifest in what is small: God "is in the greatest things, but also in the entirely small things, in our tiny, small things" (Homily, September 8, 2014). It is telling that

Francis associates God, the Almighty, with God's faithfulness, God's bond with his believing people.

Our culture has lost its sense of God's tangible presence and activity in our world. We think that God is to be found in the beyond, on another level of reality, far removed from our everyday relationships. But if this were the case, if God could not act in the world, his love would not be truly powerful, truly real, and thus not even true, a love capable of delivering the bliss that it promises. It would make no difference at all whether we believed in him or not. Christians, on the contrary, profess their faith in God's tangible and powerful love which really does act in history and determines its final destiny: a love that can be encountered, a love fully revealed in Christ's passion, death and resurrection.

—*Encyclical* Lumen Fidei, *17*

"The Lord set his love upon you and chose you" (Dt 7:7).

God is bound to us, he chose us, and this bond is forever, not so much because we are faithful, but because the Lord is faithful and endures our faithlesness, our indolence, our lapses.

God was not afraid to bind himself. This may seem odd to us: at times we call God "the Absolute," which literally means "free, independent, limitless"; but in reality our Father is always and only "absolute" in love: he made the Covenant with Abraham, with Isaac, with Jacob for love, and so forth. He loves bonds, he creates bonds; bonds that liberate, that do not restrict.

—Homily at the Gemelli Hospital in Rome, June 27, 2014

What is *the mystery in which God is hidden?* Where can I find him? All around us we see wars, the exploitation of children, torture, trafficking in arms, trafficking in persons... In all these realities, in these, the least of our brothers and sisters who are enduring these difficult situations, there is Jesus (cf. Mt 25:40, 45). The crib points us to a different path from the one cherished by the thinking of this world: it is the path of *God's self-abasement*, that humility of God's love by which he abases himself, he completely lowers himself, his glory concealed in the manger of Bethlehem, on the cross upon Calvary, in each of our suffering brothers and sisters.

—Homily for the Epiphany, January 6, 2015

... The Creator of Heaven and Earth

The God of the great history is also in the little story, because he wants to walk with each one... God is in the great things, but also in the small ones, in our small things. The Lord who walks with us is also the Lord of Patience—the patience which he had with all these generations, with all these people who lived their story of grace and sin, God is patient, God walks with us, because he wants all of us to come to be conformed to the image of his Son. And from that moment in Creation in which he gave us freedom—not independence—until today, he continues to walk with us.

—Morning Homily, September 8, 2014

You are addressing the highly complex subject of the evolution of the concept of nature. I will not go into the scientific complexity, which you well understand, of this important and crucial question. I only want to underline that God and Christ are walking with us and are also present in nature, as the apostle Paul stated in his discourse at the Areopagus: "In him we live and move and have our being" (Acts 17:28).

When we read the account of Creation in Genesis we risk imagining that God was a magician, complete with an all-powerful magic wand. But that was not so. He created beings and he let them develop according to the internal laws with which he endowed each one, that they might develop, and reach their fullness. He gave autonomy to the beings of the universe at the same time in which he assured them of his continual presence, giving life to every reality. And thus Creation has been progressing for centuries and centuries, millennia and millennia, until becoming as we know it today, precisely because God is not a demiurge or a magician, but the Creator who gives life to all beings. The beginning of the world was not a work of chaos that owes its origin to another, but derives directly from a supreme Principle who creates out of love. The Big Bang theory, which is proposed today as the origin of the world, does not contradict the intervention of a divine creator but depends on it. Evolution in nature does not conflict with the notion of Creation, because evolution presupposes the creation of beings who evolve.

As for man, however, there is a change and a novelty. When, on the sixth day in the account of Genesis, comes the moment of the creation of man, God gives the human being another autonomy, an autonomy different from that of nature, which is freedom. And he tells man to give a name to all things and to go forth through history. He makes him the steward of Creation, even that he rule over Creation, that he develop it until the end of time. Therefore the scientist, and especially the approach of the Christian scientist, is that of investigating the future of humanity and the earth, and, as a free and responsible being, to contribute to preparing it, to preserve it, and to eliminate any risks to the environment, both natural and man-made. But, at the same time, the scientist must be moved by the conviction that nature, in its evolutionary mechanisms, hides its potential which it leaves for intelligence and freedom to discover and actualize, in order to reach the development that is in the Creator's design.

So then, no matter how limited, the action of man partakes in the power of God and is capable of building a world adapted to his twofold physical and spiritual life; to build a humane world for all human beings and not only for one group or one privileged class. This hope and trust in God, the Creator of Nature, and in the capacity of the human spirit, are able to give the researcher a new impetus and profound peace. But it is also true that the action of man, when his freedom becomes autonomy—which is not freedom, but autonomy—destroys Creation and man takes the place of the Creator. And this is a grave sin against God the Creator.

—Address at the Papal Academy of Science, October 27, 2014

Even before his choice of his papal name Francis, Bergoglio had committed himself to the preservation of creation. One of the most well-known texts by Saint Francis of Assisi is his "Canticle of the Creatures" (1224), one of the earliest poems in the Italian language.

Saint Francis began the Canticle of the Creatures with these words: "Praised may you be, Most High, All-powerful God, good Lord...by all your creatures." Love for all creation, for its harmony. Saint Francis of Assisi bears witness to the need to respect all that God has created and as he created it, without manipulating and destroying creation; rather to help it grow, to become more beautiful and more like what God created it to be. And above all, Saint Francis witnesses to respect for everyone; he testifies that each of us is called to protect our neighbor, that the human person is at the center of creation, at the place where God—

our creator—willed that we should be. Not at the mercy of the idols we have created!

Harmony and peace! Saint Francis was a man of harmony and peace. From this City of Peace, I repeat with all the strength and the meekness of love: Let us respect creation, let us not be instruments of destruction! Let us respect each human being. May there be an end to armed conflicts which cover the earth with blood; may the clash of arms be silenced; and everywhere may hatred yield to love, injury to pardon, and discord to unity. Let us listen to the cry of all those who are weeping, who are suffering, and who are dying because of violence, terrorism or war... We turn to you, Francis, and we ask you: Obtain for us God's gift of harmony, peace, and respect for creation!

—Homily in Assisi, October 4, 2013

In the homily at Assisi, it is striking how the pope unites the call for peace with the history of creation. He explicitly does this as well in a prayer for freedom that he said in Saint Peter's Square in Rome in 2013.

"And God saw that it was good" (Gen 1:12, 18, 21, 25). The biblical account of the beginning of the history of the world and of humanity speaks to us of a God who looks at creation, in a sense contemplating it, and declares: "It is good." This allows us to enter into God's heart and, precisely from within him, to receive his message.

We can ask ourselves: what does this message mean? What does it say to me, to you, to all of us?

It says to us simply that this, our world, in the heart and mind of God, is the "house of harmony and peace," and that it is the space in which everyone is able to find their proper place and feel "at home, because it is good." All of creation forms a harmonious and good unity, but above all humanity, made in the image and likeness of God, is one family, in which relationships are marked by a true fraternity not only in words: the other person is a brother or sister to love, and our relationship with God, who is love, fidelity, and goodness, mirrors every human relationship and brings harmony to the whole of creation.

God's world is a world where everyone feels responsible for the other, for the good of the other. This evening, in reflection, fasting, and prayer, each of us deep down should ask ourselves: Is this really the world that I desire? Is this really the world that we all carry in our hearts? Is the world that we want really a world of harmony and peace, in ourselves, in our relations with others, in families, in cities, in and between nations? And does not true freedom mean choosing ways in this world that lead to the good of all and are guided by love?

But then we wonder: Is this the world in which we are living? Creation retains its beauty, which fills us with awe, and it remains a good work. But there is also "violence, division, disagreement, war." This occurs when man, the summit of creation, stops contemplating beauty and goodness, and withdraws into his own selfishness.

When man thinks only of himself, of his own interests, and places himself in the center, when he permits himself to be captivated by the idols of dominion and power, when he puts himself in God's place, then all relationships are broken and everything is ruined; then the door opens to violence, indifference, and conflict. This is precisely what the passage in the book of Genesis seeks to teach us in the story of the Fall: man enters into conflict with himself, he realizes that he is naked and he hides himself because he is afraid (cf. Gen 3:10), he is afraid of God's glance; he accuses the woman, she who is flesh of his flesh (cf. v. 12); he breaks harmony with creation, he begins to raise his hand against his brother to kill him. Can we say that from harmony he passes to "disharmony"? No, there is no such thing as "disharmony"; there is either harmony or we fall into chaos, where there is violence, argument, conflict, fear…

It is exactly in this chaos that God asks man's conscience: "Where is Abel your brother?" and Cain responds: "I do not know; am I my brother's keeper?" (Gen 4:9). We too are asked this question. It would be good for us to ask ourselves as well: Am I really my brother's keeper? Yes, you are your brother's keeper! To be human means to care for one another! But when harmony is broken, a metamorphosis occurs: the brother who is to be cared for and loved becomes an adversary to fight, to kill. What violence occurs at that moment, how many conflicts, how many wars have marked our history! We need only look at the suffering of so many brothers and sisters. This is not a question of coincidence, but the truth: we bring about the rebirth of Cain in every act of violence and in every war. All of us! . . .

This evening, I ask the Lord that we Christians, and our brothers and sisters of other religions, and every man and woman of good will, cry out forcefully: violence and war are never the way to peace! Let everyone be moved to look into the depths of his or her conscience and listen to that word which says: Leave behind the self-interest that hardens your heart, overcome the indifference that makes your heart insensitive toward others, conquer your deadly reasoning, and open yourself to dialogue and reconciliation. Look upon your brother's sorrow and do not add to it, stay your hand, rebuild the harmony that has been shattered; and all this achieved not by conflict but by encounter! May the noise of weapons cease! War always marks the failure of peace, it is always a defeat for humanity...

Let us pray for reconciliation and peace, let us work for reconciliation and peace, and let us all become, in every place, men and women of reconciliation and peace! Amen.

—*Prayer for Peace in the Middle East, Saint Peter's Square, September 7, 2013*

For further reflection: "Cain, where is your brother Abel?" (cf. Genesis 4:9). This is God's first question after the account of paradise in the Old Testament's book of Genesis. God's first question in general, which the Bible expresses, is similar: "Adam, where are you?" (cf. Genesis 3:9), which God addresses to Adam immediately after the fall into sin.

God ties his promise to that aspect of human life which has always appeared most "full of promise," namely, parenthood, the begetting of new life: "Sarah your wife shall bear you a son, and you shall name him Isaac" (Gen 17:19). The God who asks Abraham for complete trust reveals himself to be the source of all life. Faith is thus linked to God's fatherhood, which gives rise to all creation; the God who calls Abraham is the Creator, the one who "calls into existence the things that do not exist" (Rom 4:17), the one who "chose us before the foundation of the world . . . and destined us for adoption as his children" (Eph 1:4–5). For Abraham, faith in God sheds light on the depths of his being, it enables him to acknowledge the wellspring of goodness at the origin of all things and to realize that his life is not the product of non-being or chance, but the fruit of a personal call and a personal love. The mysterious God who called him is no alien deity, but the God who is the origin and mainstay of all that is. The great test of Abraham's faith, the sacrifice of his son Isaac, would show the extent to which this primordial love is capable of ensuring life even beyond death. The word which could raise up a son to one who was "as good as dead," in "the barrenness" of Sarah's womb (cf. Rom 4:19) can also stand by his promise of a future beyond all threat or danger (cf. Heb 11:19; Rom 4:21).

—*Encyclical* Lumen Fidei, *11*

✠

And in Jesus Christ, His Only Son, Our Lord

As a Jesuit accustomed to the Spiritual Exercises of Saint Ignatius of Loyola, Pope Francis has frequently engaged in interior reflections on the gospels. Do I walk grousing behind Jesus, or do I listen to him? Do I become impatient with his patience? Am I forming myself to be his disciple? The pope's book Open Mind, Faithful Heart: Reflections on Following Jesus *(2013) begins with the chapter "Encountering Jesus," in which Francis has assembled and analyzed many biblical accounts about the people whom Jesus encountered. "Every encounter with Jesus brings us a call, a great call or a small call, however always a call." According to the pope, not only speaking about Jesus and addressing him as "Lord" but also encountering Jesus is decisive. "Sometimes we do not see him or we do not recognize him simply because we believe that we already know him well."*

A saint used to say: "I am afraid that the Lord will come." Do you know what the fear was? It was the fear of not noticing and letting him pass by. When we feel in our hearts: "I would like to be a better man, a better woman . . . I regret what I have done," that is the Lord knocking. He makes you feel this: the will to be better, the will to be closer to others, to God. If you feel this, stop. That is the Lord! And go to prayer, and maybe to confession, cleanse yourselves . . . this will be good. But keep well in mind: if you feel this longing to be better, he is knocking: don't let him pass by!

—*Angelus Prayer, December 21, 2014*

In hardly any other text has Pope Francis so energetically interacted with the so-called historical Jesus as in his letter to the (non-believing) journalist and publicist Eugenio Scalfari. In order to come to his faith-based understanding of Jesus, Francis proceeds from Mark's gospel and is caught up in the question of Jesus' contemporaries concerning whose "power" Jesus employs (cf. Mark 3:22–27). Most significant in his letter to Scalfari is how Pope Francis clearly brings into this consideration his own relationship with Jesus in the Church. And his answer to the question of the originality of the Christian faith is original, in the best sense of the word.

For me, faith was born of an encounter with Jesus. It was a personal encounter that touched my heart and gave new direction and meaning to my life. At the same time, it was an encounter made possible by the community of faith in which I lived and thanks to which I gained access to understanding sacred scripture, to new life in Christ through the sacraments, to fraternity with all and service to the poor, who are the true image of the Lord. Without the Church—believe me—I would not have been able to encounter Jesus, even with the awareness that the immense gift of faith is kept in the fragile clay jars of our humanity...

From this personal experience of faith lived in the Church, I find myself able to listen to your questions and, with you, to seek the paths along which we may walk together...

It is necessary... to look at Jesus from the point of view of the actual circumstances of his existence, as narrated by the oldest of the gospels, Saint Mark. There, the "scandal" in others, provoked by the words and actions of Jesus, stems from his extraordinary "authority." This word, present already in the gospel of Saint Mark, is not easy to translate accurately in Italian. The Greek word is *exousia,* which etymologically refers to that which "comes from being," from whom one is. It is not something external or imposed, but rather that which comes from within and is self-evident. Jesus, in fact, impacts us, shocks us, and renews us, and this comes, as he himself says, from his relationship with God, whom he refers to intimately as *Abba*, the Father, who confers this "authority" upon him so that he may offer it for humanity's sake.

In this way, Jesus preaches "as one who has authority"; he heals, he calls the disciples to follow him, he forgives, all of which are realities that in the Old Testament come only from God. The question that arises repeatedly in the gospel of Mark, "Who is this that . . . ?" concerning the identity of Jesus, arises from the recognition of an authority that is not of this world, one which is not intended to impose itself on others but rather is directed to the service of others, to give them freedom and fullness of life. And this he did even to the extent of risking his own life, of experiencing incomprehension, betrayal, rejection, to the point of being condemned to death, to the point of plummeting into the depths of abandonment on the cross. Yet Jesus remained faithful to God, to the end.

It is precisely at this moment—as the Roman centurion exclaims at the foot of the cross in Saint Mark's gospel—that Jesus reveals himself, paradoxically, as the Son of God, the Son of a God who is love and who desires, with his whole being, that all men and women discover themselves and live as his true children. For the Christian faith, this is confirmed by the fact that Jesus is risen; not to bring the weight of his triumph to bear on those who have rejected him, but to show that the love of God is stronger than death, that the forgiveness of God is stronger than any sin, and that it is worth giving one's life to the end in order to bear witness to this immense gift . . .

Returning to the editorial of July 7, you ask me furthermore how to understand the unique identity of the Christian faith inasmuch as it centers on the incarnation of the Son of God, with respect to other faiths that rest on the absolute transcendence of God.

The uniqueness lies, I would say, in the fact that the faith makes us share, through Jesus, in the relationship he has with God who is *Abba,* and from this perspective, in the relationship of love which he has with all men and women, enemies included. In other words, the sonship of Jesus, as presented by the Christian faith, is not revealed so as to emphasize an insurmountable separation between Jesus and everyone else; rather, it is revealed to tell us that, in him, we are all called to be children of the one Father and so brothers and sisters to one another. The uniqueness of Jesus has to do with communication, not exclusion.

—Letter to a Nonbeliever, Eugenio Scalfari, September 11, 2013

Jesus praises the Father because he has hidden the things of God from the learned and revealed them to little ones. To understand God's love you need that littleness of heart. Besides, Jesus tells us clearly: if you don't become like children you will not enter the kingdom of heaven. That's the right way: become children, become little, because only in that littleness, in that self-lowering, can you receive God's love.

It's not accidental, when he explains how he loves, that the Lord himself tries to speak as if talking to a child. God reminds the people: "Remember, I taught you to walk as a father teaches his child." It's about that father-child relationship. But, if you don't become little, that relationship can't happen.

It's a relationship that leads the Lord in his love for us to use words that are like a lullaby. For in the Bible the Lord says: "Don't be afraid, little grub of Israel, don't be afraid!" And he touches us tenderly telling us: I am with you, I take you by the hand.

That's the Lord's loving tenderness, that's what he shares with us. It also empowers our own tenderness. But if we think of ourselves as strong, we will never experience the beauty of the Lord's tenderness.

The Lord's words make us understand the mysterious love he has for us. Jesus himself shows us what to do. When he speaks about himself, he says he is "gentle and humble of heart." So he too, God's son, humbles himself to receive the Father's love.

—Morning Homily, June 27, 2014

Dear brothers and sisters, in Christ we contemplate God's faithfulness. Every act, every word of Jesus reveals the merciful and steadfast love of the Father. And so before him we ask ourselves: how is my love for my neighbor? Do I know how to be faithful? Or am I inconsistent, following my moods and impulses? Each of us can answer in our own mind. But above all we can say to the Lord: Lord

Jesus, render my heart ever more like yours, full of love and faithfulness.

—Homily at the Gemelli Hospital in Rome, June 27, 2014

If Jesus is not at the center, other things are. And today we find so many Christians without Christ, without Jesus. For example, [there are] those who have the Pharisees' disease and are Christians who express their faith, their religiosity, their Christianity, in so many commandments: Oh, I've got to do this, I've got to do that. Duty Christians—that is to say, they do things because they have to do them, but really they don't know why they're doing them."

But where is Jesus? A commandment is valid if it comes from Jesus. There are so many Christians without Christ, like those who only go in for devotions, so many devotions, but Jesus isn't there. So then you're missing something, brother! You're missing Jesus. If your devotions lead you to Jesus, then fine. But if you just stay where you are, then something isn't right.

So what is the rule for being a Christian with Christ? And what is the sign that someone is a Christian with Christ? There's one very simple rule: only what brings you to Jesus is valid, and only what comes from Jesus is valid. Jesus is the center, the Lord, as he himself says.

So if something leads to or comes from Jesus, go ahead. But if it doesn't come from or lead to Jesus then it's rather dangerous. A man or woman who worships Jesus is a

Christian with Jesus. But if you can't worship Jesus, then something's missing in you.

So here's a rule and a sign. The rule is this: I'm a good Christian, I'm on the right road to be a good Christian, if I do what comes from Jesus or what leads me to Jesus, because he's the center. The sign is worshiping Jesus, worshiping Jesus in prayer.

—Morning Homily, September 7, 2013

Paul said of himself: "I boast only of my sins." These were scandalous words. In another verse he says: "I boast only of Christ and of his Cross." Thus, the strength of God's Word is in that encounter between my sins and the blood of Christ who saves me. And when there is no such encounter, there is no strength in the heart. And when we forget that encounter, we become worldly, we want to speak about the matters of God with human language, and this is useless, because it is not life giving.

The privileged place for the encounter with Jesus Christ is one's sins. If a Christian is incapable of feeling himself a sinner and saved by the blood of Christ crucified, he is a half-way Christian, he is a tepid Christian. When we find decadent churches, when we find decadent parishes, decadent institutions, certainly the Christians who are there have never encountered Jesus Christ, or they have forgotten that encounter with Jesus Christ.

The strength of the Christian life and the strength of the Word of God lie precisely in that moment where I, a sinner, encounter Jesus Christ. And that encounter turns life inside-out; it is life changing. And it gives you the strength to proclaim salvation to others.

—Morning Homily, September 4, 2014

We can ask, what is our identity as Christians? Paul says it well: "We impart this in words not taught by human wisdom." Paul's preaching does not emanate from human wisdom, because his words were taught to him by the Holy Spirit. In fact, he preached with the anointing of the Spirit, expressing spiritual matters of the Spirit in spiritual terms...

Now we have the mind of Christ, that is, the Spirit of Christ. And this is the Christian identity: not having the spirit of the world, that manner of thinking, that manner of judging.

Ultimately, what gives authority, what gives identity is the Holy Spirit, the anointing of the Holy Spirit. This is why people didn't love those preachers, those legal experts, because they spoke truly about theology but they didn't reach the heart, they didn't give freedom, they weren't capable of doing so in a manner the people identified with, because they were not anointed by the Holy Spirit. However, the authority of Jesus—and the authority of the Christian—comes from this very capacity to understand the gifts of the Spirit, to speak the language of the Spirit; it comes from this anointing of the Holy Spirit.

—Morning Homily, September 2, 2014

Jesus turns to us and asks us the same question he put to Peter: Who am I? Who is Jesus Christ for each one of us, for me? Who is Jesus Christ? In order to reply to that question we all hear in our hearts it is not enough to repeat what we've learned in the catechism. Of course it's important to study the catechism and get to know it, but it isn't enough, because to know him truly it's necessary to make the journey Peter made. Indeed, after that humiliation (Jesus has told him shortly after his messianic confession: "Get behind me Satan"), Peter carried on with Jesus, he saw the miracles Jesus performed, he saw his powers.

But at a certain point Peter denied Jesus, he betrayed Jesus. At that very moment he learned that difficult knowledge—wisdom rather than knowledge—of tears, of weeping. Peter asked the Lord for forgiveness.

So the question to Peter—who am I for you?—can be understood only by making a long journey, a journey of grace and sin, the journey of a disciple. For Jesus didn't say to Peter or his other apostles: Know me! He said: Follow me! And it's by following Jesus that we get to know Jesus. Following Jesus with our virtues and also with our sins, but always following Jesus!

To know Jesus, it isn't necessary to study ideas, but to live as a disciple. In that way, by walking with Jesus, we learn who he is, we learn the knowledge of Jesus. We get know Jesus as his disciples did. We get to know him by meeting daily with the Lord, with our daily victories and our weaknesses. It's through those meetings that we come close to him and get to know him more deeply. Because in those everyday meetings we get what Paul calls the mind of Christ.

We get to know Jesus as disciples on the road of life by following him. But that isn't enough, because knowing Jesus is a gift from the Father: it is he who enables us to know Jesus. Really, it's a work of the Holy Spirit. And he's always working in us and he does that great work of explaining the mystery of Jesus and giving us the mind of Christ.

As disciples of Jesus, let us ask the Father to give us the knowledge of Christ and the Holy Spirit to explain this mystery to us.

—*Morning Homily, February 20, 2014*

☩ *For further reflection: "But who do you say I am?" (cf. Mark 8:29).*

Faith does not merely gaze at Jesus, but sees things as Jesus himself sees them, with his own eyes: it is a participation in his way of seeing. In many areas in our lives we trust others who know more than we do… Christ's life, his way of knowing the Father and living in complete and constant relationship with him, opens up new and inviting vistas for human experience… To enable us to know, accept, and follow him, the Son of God took on our flesh. In this way he also saw the Father humanly, within the setting of a journey unfolding in time.

Christian faith is faith in the incarnation of the Word and his bodily resurrection; it is faith in a God who is so close to us that he entered our human history. Far from divorcing us from reality, our faith in the Son of God made man in Jesus of Nazareth enables us to grasp reality's deepest meaning and to see how much God loves this world and is constantly guiding it toward himself. This leads us, as Christians, to live our lives in this world with ever greater commitment and intensity.

—*Encyclical* Lumen Fidei, *18*

For further reflection: "The Christian faith looks not only at Jesus, but it also looks out from the perspective of Jesus, seeing with his eyes." An interesting change in perspectives. Who comes into view when I look at the world with Jesus' eyes?

It was only in this way, by taking flesh, by sharing our humanity, that the knowledge proper to love could come to full fruition... By his taking flesh and coming among us, Jesus has touched us, and through the sacraments he continues to touch us even today; transforming our hearts, he unceasingly enables us to acknowledge and acclaim him as the Son of God. In faith, we can touch him and receive the power of his grace.

—*Encyclical* Lumen Fidei, *31*

... Who Was Conceived by the Holy Spirit

Pope Francis comments in an entirely understandable manner on this statement of faith concerning the Holy Spirit. In this, there results a point of contact with his often expressed conviction that God is a "God of surprises," and that our encounter with God occurs not through our actions, deeds, or organization but when we allow God's surprises to occur—as Mary did (cf. Luke 1:26–38). Concerning Saint Joseph, Mary's husband, Francis speaks with moving words; in his sermon to church officials he characterizes Joseph as "protector."

How does Joseph respond to his calling to be the protector of Mary, Jesus and the Church? By being constantly attentive to God, open to the signs of God's presence, and receptive to God's plans and not simply to his own... Joseph is a "protector" because he is able to hear God's voice and be guided by his will... In him, dear friends, we learn how to respond to God's call, readily and willingly, but we also see the core of the Christian vocation, which is Christ!

—Inaugural Homily, March 19, 2013

The Virgin Mary teaches us what it means to live in the Holy Spirit and what it means to accept the news of God in our life. She conceived Jesus by the work of the Holy Spirit, and every Christian, each one of us, is called to accept the Word of God, to accept Jesus inside of us and then to bring him to everyone... May Mary help you to be attentive to what the Lord asks of you, and to live and walk forever with the Holy Spirit!

— Angelus Prayer, April 28, 2013

Allow yourselves to be surprised by God. Anyone who is a man or a woman of hope—the great hope which faith gives us—knows that even in the midst of difficulties God acts and he surprises us... God always surprises us, like the new wine in the gospel we have just heard. God always saves the best for us. But he asks us to let ourselves be surprised by his love, to accept his surprises. Let us trust God!

—Sermon in Aparecida, Brazil, June 24, 2013

Truly, God surprises us. It is precisely in poverty, in weakness, and in humility that he reveals himself and grants us his love, which saves us, heals us, and gives us strength. He asks us only to obey his word and to trust in him. This was the experience of the Virgin Mary. At the message of the angel, she does not hide her surprise. It was the astonishment of realizing that God, to become man, had chosen her, a simple maid of Nazareth. Not someone who lived in a palace amid power and riches, or one who had done extraordinary things, but simply someone who was open to God and put her trust in him, even without understanding everything: "Here I am, the servant of the Lord; let it be with me according to your word" (Lk 1:38). That was her answer. God constantly surprises us, he bursts our categories, he wreaks havoc with our plans. And he tells us: Trust me, do not be afraid, let yourself be surprised, leave yourself behind and follow me!

Today let us all ask ourselves whether we are afraid of what God might ask, or of what he does ask. Do I let myself be surprised by God, as Mary was, or do I remain caught up in my own safety zone: in forms of material, intellectual, or ideological security, taking refuge in my own projects and plans? Do I truly let God into my life? How do I answer him?...

Take Mary. After the Annunciation, her first act is one of charity toward her elderly kinswoman Elizabeth. Her first words are: "My soul magnifies the Lord," in other words, a song of praise and thanksgiving to God not only for what he has done for her, but for what he has done throughout the history of salvation. Everything is his gift. If we can realize that everything is God's gift, how happy will our hearts be! Everything is his gift. He is our strength!

—Sermon for Marian Day, October 13, 2013

Everything is a free gift from God, everything is grace, everything is a gift out of his love for us. The Angel Gabriel calls Mary "full of grace" (Lk 1:28): in her there is no room for sin, because God chose her from eternity to be the mother of Jesus and preserved her from original sin. And Mary corresponds to the grace and abandons herself, saying to the angel: "Let it be done to me according to your word" (v. 38). She does not say: "I shall do it according to your word": no! But: "Let it be done to me..." And the Word was made flesh in her womb. We too are asked to listen to God who speaks to us, and to accept his will. According to the logic of the gospel nothing is more productive and fruitful than listening to and accepting the Word of the Lord, which comes from the gospel, from the Bible. The Lord is always speaking to us!

The attitude of Mary of Nazareth shows us that *being* comes before *doing*, and [that we need] *to leave the doing* to God in order *to be* truly as he wants us. It is he who works so many marvels in us. Mary is receptive, but not passive because, on the physical level, she receives the power of the Holy Spirit and then gives flesh and blood to the Son of God who forms within her. Thus, on the spiritual level, she accepts the grace and corresponds to it with faith. That is why Saint Augustine affirms that the Virgin "conceived in her heart before her womb" (*Discourses*, 215, 4). She conceived first faith and then the Lord. This mystery of the acceptance of grace, which in Mary, as a unique privilege, was without the obstacle of sin, is a possibility for all...

Regarding this love, regarding this mercy, the divine grace poured into our hearts, one single thing is asked in return: unreserved giving. Not one of us can buy salvation! Salvation is a free gift of the Lord, a free gift of God that comes within us and dwells in us. As we have received freely, so are we called to give freely (cf. Mt 10:8); imitating Mary, who, immediately upon receiving the Angel's announcement, went to share the gift of her fruitfulness with her relative Elizabeth. Because if everything has been given to us, then everything must be passed on. How? By allowing that the Holy Spirit make of us a gift for others. The Spirit is a gift for us and we, by the power of the Spirit, must be a gift for others and allow the Holy Spirit to turn us into instruments of acceptance, instruments of reconciliation, instruments of forgiveness.

— *Angelus Prayer, December 8, 2014*

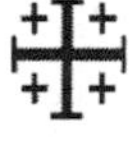

For further reflection: Do I allow God to act, or do I want to do everything myself?

... Born of the Virgin Mary

The Christian faith professes that Jesus is the Son of God who came to give his life to open the way of love to all people. Thus you are correct, Dr. Scalfari, when you recognize that the Christian faith hinges on the incarnation of the Son of God. Tertullian wrote *"caro cardo salutis,"* the flesh (of Christ) is the fulcrum of salvation. Because the incarnation, the Son of God coming in our flesh and sharing the joys and sorrows, the successes and failures of our life, even to cry-ing out on the cross, experiencing all things with love and fidelity to *Abba*, testifies to the astonishing love of God for all people, and to the inestimable worth that he sees in them. On account of this, each one of us is called to make Christ's gaze and love his own, and to enter into his way of being, of thinking, and of acting.

—Letter to a Nonbeliever, Eugenio Scalfari, September 11, 2013

Francis would not be Francis if he did not repeatedly give prominence to the birth of Jesus. He stresses that God's Son entered into life in the unapparent, in poverty, and on the periphery of the world. Of this, the following texts speak. In his sermon in Bethlehem the pope emphasizes that the divine sign to the shepherds happens not in a demonstration of power but when the shepherds find a defenseless, small child.

The Incarnation of the Son of God opens a new beginning in the universal history of man and woman. And this new beginning happens within a family, in Nazareth. Jesus was born in a family. He could have come in a spectacular way, or as a warrior, an emperor... No, no: he is born in a family, in a family. This is important: to perceive in the nativity this beautiful scene.

God chose to come into the world in a human family, which he himself formed. He formed it in a remote village on the outskirts of the Roman Empire. Not in Rome, which was the capital of the empire, not in a big city, but on its nearly invisible outskirts, indeed, of little renown. The gospels also recall this, almost as an expression: "Can anything good come out of Nazareth?" (Jn 1:46). Perhaps, in many parts of the world, we still talk this way, when we hear the name of some areas on the periphery of a big city. And so, right there, on the outskirts of the great empire, began the most holy and good story of Jesus among men!

—General Audience, December 17, 2014

God's grace has been revealed, and it has made salvation possible for the whole human race" (Tit 2:11). The grace which was revealed in our world is Jesus, born of the Virgin Mary, true man and true God. He has entered our history; he has shared our journey. He came to free us from darkness and to grant us light. In him was revealed the grace, the mercy, and the tender love of the Father: Jesus is Love incarnate. He is not simply a teacher of wisdom, he is not an ideal for which we strive while knowing that we are hopelessly distant from it. He is the meaning of life and history who has pitched his tent in our midst.

The shepherds were the first to see this "tent," to receive the news of Jesus' birth. They were the first because they were among the last, the outcast. And they were the first because they were awake, keeping watch in the night, guarding their flocks. The pilgrim is bound by duty to keep watch and the shepherds did just that. Together with them, let us pause before the Child, let us pause in silence.

Together with them, let us thank the Lord for having given Jesus to us, and with them let us raise from the depths of our hearts the praises of his fidelity: We bless you, Lord God most high, who lowered yourself for our sake. You are immense, and you made yourself small; you are rich and you made yourself poor; you are all-powerful and you made yourself vulnerable.

—*Sermon for Midnight Mass, December 24, 2013*

"This will be a sign for you: you will find a child wrapped in swaddling clothes and lying in a manger" (Lk 2:12)... The Child Jesus, born in Bethlehem, is the *sign* given by God to those who awaited salvation, and he remains forever the sign of God's tenderness and presence in our world. The angel announces to the shepherds: "This will be a sign for you: you will find a child..."

To us, the men and women of the twenty-first century, God today also says: "This will be a sign for you," look to the child... The Child of Bethlehem is frail, like all newborn children. He cannot speak and yet he is the Word made flesh who came to transform the hearts and lives of all men and women. This Child, like every other child, is vulnerable; he needs to be accepted and protected. Today too, children need to be welcomed and defended, from the moment of their conception...

And we have to ask ourselves: Who are we, as we stand before the Child Jesus? Who are we, standing as we stand before today's children? Are we like Mary and Joseph, who welcomed Jesus and cared for him with the love of a father and a mother? Or are we like Herod, who wanted to eliminate him? Are we like the shepherds, who went in haste to kneel before him in worship and offer him their humble gifts? Or are we indifferent? Are we perhaps people who use fine and pious words, yet exploit pictures of poor children in order to make money? Are we ready to be there for children, to "waste time" with them? Are we ready to listen to them, to care for them, to pray for them and with them?...

Mary, Mother of Jesus, you who accepted, teach us how to accept; you who adored, teach us how to adore; you who followed, teach us how to follow. Amen.

—Sermon in Bethlehem, May 25, 2014

We abiding in God and God abiding in us. Christian life *is* this double "abiding." But not abiding in the spirit of the world. Not abiding in superficiality, not abiding in idolatry, not abiding in vanity. No, abiding in the Lord! And, the Lord "returns this and so he too abides in us. Or rather, he first abides in us but we so often chase him away and so we can't abide in him...

The criterion of abiding in the Lord and the Lord in us and the criterion of Christian embodied concreteness is always the same: the Word became flesh. The criterion is faith in the incarnation of the Word, God become man. There's no true Christianity without this foundation. The key to

Christian life is faith in Jesus Christ, God's Word become human.

But be aware that the love John is speaking of isn't love like in a soap opera! No, it's something else! Actually, Christian love always has a certain quality: embodiment. Christian love is palpable and practical. When Jesus himself speaks of love, he speaks about palpable, practical things: feeding the hungry, visiting the sick. These are all practical things, because love is palpable and practical. That's Christian practicality. When that practicality is lacking, we end up with a disembodied Christianity based on illusions, because we fail to understand the central message of Jesus. Love that isn't palpable and practical becomes love based on illusions. It was also an illusion which the disciples had when they saw Jesus and thought he was a ghost.

There's a question each of us must ask ourselves: If I abide in Jesus, abide in the Lord, abide in love, what do I do—not what do I think or what do I say—for God, or what do I do for others? The first criterion is to love by deeds, not words... The second criterion for being palpable and practical is that in loving it's more important to give than to receive.

The one and only criterion for abiding is our faith in Jesus Christ, God's Word made flesh.

—Morning Homily, January 9, 2014

For further reflection: The Incarnation, the "Christian concreteness."

Mother and Son were together, just as they were together at Calvary, because *Christ and his mother are inseparable*. There is a very close relationship between them, as there is between every child and his or her mother. The flesh (*caro*) of Christ—which, as Tertullian says, is the hinge (*cardo*) of our salvation—was knit together in the womb of Mary (cf. Ps 139:13). This inseparability is also clear from the fact that Mary, chosen beforehand to be the mother of the Redeemer, shared intimately in his entire mission, remaining at her Son's side to the end on Calvary.

Mary is so closely united to Jesus because she received from him the knowledge of the heart, the knowledge of faith, nourished by her experience as a mother and by her close relationship with her Son. The Blessed Virgin is the woman of faith who made room for God in her heart and in her plans; she is the believer capable of perceiving in the gift of her Son the coming of that "fullness of time" (Gal 4:4) in which God, by choosing the humble path of human existence, entered personally into the history of salvation. That is why Jesus cannot be understood without his Mother.

—Sermon for the Solemnity of Mary, Mother of God, January 1, 2015

For further reflection: From the pope's words about Mary there unfolds a definition of Christian faith: "To believe means to give God room in my heart, in my plans."

When the angels announced the birth of the Redeemer to the shepherds, they did so with these words: "This will be a sign for you: you will find a baby wrapped in swaddling clothes and lying in a manger" (Lk 2:12). The "sign" is in fact the humility of God, the humility of God taken to the extreme. It is the love with which, that night, he assumed our frailty, our suffering, our anxieties, our desires, and our limitations. The message that everyone was expecting, that everyone was searching for in the depths of their souls, was none other than the tenderness of God: God who looks upon us with eyes full of love, who accepts our poverty, God who is in love with our smallness.

On this holy night, while we contemplate the Infant Jesus just born and placed in the manger, we are invited to reflect. How do we welcome the tenderness of God? Do I allow myself to be taken up by God, to be embraced by him, or do I prevent him from drawing close? "But I am searching for the Lord"—we could respond. Nevertheless, what is most important is not seeking him, but rather allowing him to seek me, find me, and caress me with tenderness. The question put to us simply by the Infant's presence is: Do I allow God to love me?

Further, do we have the courage to welcome with tenderness the difficulties and problems of those who are near to us, or do we prefer impersonal solutions, perhaps effective but devoid of the warmth of the gospel? How much the world needs tenderness today! The patience of God, the closeness of God, the tenderness of God.

The Christian response cannot be different from God's response to our smallness. Life must be met with goodness, with meekness. When we realize that God is in love with our smallness, that he made himself small in order to better encounter us, we cannot help but open our hearts to him, and beseech him: "Lord, help me to be like you, give me the grace of tenderness in the most difficult circumstances of life, give me the grace of closeness in the face of every need, of meekness in every conflict."

—Sermon for Midnight Mass, December 24, 2014

For further reflection: God is "enamored with our small existence."

. . . Suffered under Pontius Pilate, Was Crucified, Died and Was Buried

No Christian Belief without the Cross

On the morning after his election, Francis delivered to the cardinals his first sermon as pope. Unlike the popes who preceded him, he did not outline his "plan of governance." Rather, he gave a freely formulated meditation on going forward, on the building up of the Church, and on confessing the crucified Lord. In particular, the new pope spoke with intensity about the central significance of the cross of Christ.

We can walk as much as we want, we can build many things, but if we do not profess Jesus Christ, things go wrong. We may become a charitable NGO, but not the Church, the Bride of the Lord. When we are not walking, we stop moving. When we are not building on the stones, what happens? The same thing that happens to children on the beach when they build sandcastles: everything is swept away, there is no solidity. When we do not profess Jesus Christ, the saying of Léon Bloy comes to mind: "Anyone who does not pray to the Lord prays to the devil." When we do not profess Jesus Christ, we profess the worldliness of the devil, a demonic worldliness.

Journeying, building, professing. But things are not so straightforward, because in journeying, building, professing, there can sometimes be jolts, movements that are not properly part of the journey, movements that pull us back.

This gospel continues with a situation of a particular kind. The same Peter who professed Jesus Christ now says to him: You are the Christ, the Son of the living God. I will follow you, but let us not speak of the cross. That has nothing to do with it. I will follow you on other terms, but without the cross. When we journey without the cross, when we build without the cross, when we profess Christ without the cross, we are not disciples of the Lord, we are worldly: we may be bishops, priests, cardinals, popes, but not disciples of the Lord.

My wish is that all of us, after these days of grace, will have the courage, yes, the courage, to walk in the presence of the Lord, with the Lord's cross; to build the Church on the Lord's blood which was poured out on the cross; and to profess the one glory: Christ crucified. And in this way, the Church will go forward.

—First Sermon as Pope, Sistine Chapel, March 14, 2013

Faith in Jesus Christ is not a joke, it is something very serious. It is a scandal that God came to be one of us. It is a scandal that he died on a cross. It is a scandal: the scandal of the cross. The cross continues to provoke scandal. But it is the one sure path, the path of the cross, the path of Jesus, the path of the Incarnation of Jesus. Please do not water down your faith in Jesus Christ. We dilute fruit drinks—orange, apple, or banana juice—but please do not drink a diluted form of faith. Faith is whole and entire, not something that you water down. It is faith in Jesus. It is faith in the Son of God made man, who loved me and who died for me.

—Address to Argentinian youth in Rio de Janeiro, July 25, 2013

Beginning with the newly baptized, we are all Church, and we must all follow the path of Jesus, who himself took the road of renunciation. He became a servant, one who serves; he chose to be humiliated even to the cross. And if we want to be Christians, there is no other way. But can't we make Christianity a little more human—they say—without the cross, without Jesus, without renunciation? In this way we would become like Christians in a pastry shop, saying:

What beautiful cakes, what beautiful sweets! Truly beautiful, but not really Christians! Someone could ask: "Of what must the Church divest herself?" Today she must strip herself of a very grave danger, which threatens every person in the Church, everyone: the danger of worldliness. The Christian cannot coexist with the spirit of the world, with the worldliness that leads us to vanity, to arrogance, to pride. And this is an idol, it is not God. It is an idol! And idolatry is the gravest of sins!

When the media speaks about the Church, they believe the Church is made up of priests, sisters, bishops, cardinals and the pope. But we are all the Church, as I said. And we all must strip ourselves of this worldliness: the spirit opposing the spirit of the Beatitudes, the spirit opposing the spirit of Jesus. Worldliness hurts us. It is so very sad to find a worldly Christian, sure—according to him—of that security that the faith gives and of the security that the world provides. You cannot be on both sides. The Church—all of us—must strip herself of the worldliness that leads to vanity, to pride, that is idolatry.

—Speaking to the poor in Assisi, October 4, 2013

Christianity is not a philosophical doctrine, it is not a program of life that enables one to be well formed and to make peace. These are its consequences. Christianity is a person, a person lifted up on the cross. A person who emptied himself to save us. He took on sin. Therefore, one cannot understand Christianity without understanding this profound humiliation of the Son of God, who humbled himself and made himself a servant unto death on the cross.

And that is why there is no Christianity without the cross, and there is no cross without Jesus Christ. The heart of God's salvation is his Son who took upon himself our sins, our pride, our self-reliance, our vanity, our desire to be like God. A Christian who is not able to glory in Christ crucified has not understood what it means to be Christian. Our wounds, those which sin leaves in us, are healed only through the Lord's wounds, through the wounds of God made man who humbled himself, who emptied himself. This is the mystery of the cross. It is not only an ornament that we always put in churches, on the altar; it is not only a symbol that should distinguish us from others. The cross is a mystery: the mystery of the love of God who humbles himself, who empties himself to save us from our sins.

Where is your sin? Your sin is there on the cross. Go and look for it there, in the wounds of the Lord, and your sins shall be healed, your wounds shall be healed, your sins shall be forgiven. God's forgiveness is not a matter of canceling a debt we have with him. God forgives us in the wounds of his Son lifted up on the cross. May the Lord draw us to himself that we might allow ourselves to be healed.

—Morning Homily, April 8, 2014

For further reflection: Do I know that I should "boast of the crucified Christ"? What does the cross mean for me? Does a cross hang on my wall? Do I notice it?

Am I Judas or Pilate?

The following text is a typical Jesuit examination of conscience, as Pope Francis has many times freely formulated it without speaking from a prepared sermon. Where do I stand in the passion narrative?

We have just listened to the Passion of our Lord. We might well ask ourselves just one question: Who am I? Who am I, before my Lord? Who am I, before Jesus who enters Jerusalem amid the enthusiasm of the crowd? Am I ready to express my joy, to praise him? Or do I stand back? Who am I, before the suffering Jesus?

We have just heard many, many names. The group of leaders, some priests, the Pharisees, the teachers of the law, who had decided to kill Jesus. They were waiting for the chance to arrest him. Am I like one of them?

We have also heard another name: Judas. Thirty pieces of silver. Am I like Judas? We have heard other names too: the disciples who understood nothing, who fell asleep while the Lord was suffering. Has my life fallen asleep? Or am I like the disciples, who did not realize what it was to betray Jesus? Or like that other disciple, who wanted to settle everything with a sword? Am I like them? Am I like Judas, who feigns love and then kisses the Master in order to hand him over, to betray him? Am I a traitor? Am I like those people in power who hastily summon a tribunal and seek false witnesses? Am I like them? And when I do these things, if I do them, do I think that in this way I am saving the people?

Am I like Pilate? When I see that the situation is difficult, do I wash my hands and dodge my responsibility, allowing people to be condemned—or condemning them myself?

Am I like that crowd which was not sure whether they were at a religious meeting, a trial, or a circus, and then chose Barabbas? For them it was all the same: it was more entertaining to humiliate Jesus.

Am I like the soldiers who strike the Lord, spit on him, insult him, who find entertainment in humiliating him?

Am I like the Cyrenean, who was returning from work, weary, yet was good enough to help the Lord carry his cross?

Am I like those who walked by the cross and mocked Jesus: "He was so courageous? Let him come down from the cross and then we will believe in him!" Mocking Jesus...

Am I like those fearless women, and like the mother of Jesus, who were there, and who suffered in silence?

Am I like Joseph, the hidden disciple, who lovingly carried the body of Jesus to give it burial?

Am I like the two Marys, who remained at the tomb, weeping and praying?

Am I like those leaders who went the next day to Pilate and said, "Look, this man said that he was going to rise again. We cannot let another fraud take place!" and who block life, who block the tomb, in order to maintain doctrine, lest life come forth?

Where is my heart? Which of these persons am I like?

—*Sermon for Palm Sunday, April 13, 2014*

"He came out and went . . . to the Mount of Olives; and the disciples followed him" (Lk 22:39). At the hour which God had appointed to save humanity from its enslavement to sin, Jesus came here, to Gethsemane, to the foot of the Mount of Olives. We now find ourselves in this holy place, a place sanctified by the prayer of Jesus, by his agony, by his sweating of blood, and above all by his "yes" to the loving will of the Father. We dread in some sense to approach what Jesus went through at that hour; we tread softly as we enter that inner space where the destiny of the world was decided.

In that hour, Jesus felt the need to pray and to have with him his disciples, his friends, those who had followed him and shared most closely in his mission. But here, at Gethsemane, following him became difficult and uncertain. They were overcome by doubt, weariness and fright. As the events of Jesus' passion rapidly unfolded, the disciples would adopt different attitudes before the Master: attitudes of closeness, distance, hesitation.

Here, in this place, each of us might do well to ask: Who am I, before the sufferings of my Lord? Am I among those who, when Jesus asks them to keep watch with him, fall asleep instead, and rather than praying, seek to escape, refusing to face reality? Or do I see myself in those who fled out of fear, who abandoned the Master at the most tragic hour in his earthly life?...Do I see myself in those who drew back and denied him, like Peter?...Or, thanks be to God, do I find myself among those who remained faithful to the end, like the Virgin Mary and the apostle John? On Golgotha, when everything seemed bleak and all hope seemed pointless, only love proved stronger than death. The love of the Mother and the beloved disciple made them stay at the foot of the cross, sharing in the pain of Jesus to the very end...Let us imitate the Virgin Mary and Saint John, and stand by all those crosses where Jesus continues to be crucified. This is how the Lord calls us to follow him: this is the path, there is no other!

—Address at the Mount of Olives in Jerusalem, May 26, 2014

The Cross: God's Answer

I do not wish to add too many words. One word should suffice this evening, that is the cross itself. The cross is the word through which God has responded to evil in the world. Sometimes it may seem as though God does not react to evil, as if he is silent. And yet, God has spoken, he has replied, and his answer is the cross of Christ: a word which is love, mercy, forgiveness. It is also reveals a judgment, namely that God, in judging us, loves us. Let us remember this: God judges us by loving us. If I embrace his love then I am saved, if I refuse it, then I am condemned, not by him, but my own self, because God never condemns, he only loves and saves.

Dear brothers and sisters, the word of the cross is also the answer which Christians offer in the face of evil, the evil that continues to work in us and around us. Christians must respond to evil with good, taking the cross upon themselves as Jesus did. This evening we have heard the witness given by our Lebanese brothers and sisters: they composed these beautiful prayers and meditations. We extend our heartfelt gratitude to them for this work and for the witness they offer. We were able to see this when Pope Benedict visited Lebanon. We saw the beauty and the strong bond of communion joining Christians together in that land and the friendship of our Muslim brothers and sisters and so many others. That occasion was a sign to the Middle East and to the whole world: a sign of hope.

We now continue this *Via Crucis* in our daily lives. Let us walk together along the Way of the Cross and let us do so carrying in our hearts this word of love and forgiveness. Let us go forward waiting for the resurrection of Jesus, who loves us so much. He is all love!

—The Way of the Cross at Rome's Colosseum on Good Friday, March 29, 2013

God placed on Jesus' cross all the weight of our sins, all the injustices perpetrated by every Cain against his brother, all the bitterness of the betrayal by Judas and by Peter, all the vanity of tyrants, all the arrogance of false friends. It was a heavy cross, like night experienced by abandoned people, heavy like the death of loved ones, heavy because it carries all the ugliness of evil.

However, the cross is also glorious like the dawn after a long night, for it represents the love of God, which is greater than our iniquities and our betrayals. In the cross we see the monstrosity of man when he allows evil to guide him; but we also see the immensity of the mercy of God, who does not treat us according to our sins but according to his mercy.

Before the cross of Jesus, we apprehend in a way that we can almost touch with our hands how much we are eternally loved; before the cross we feel that we are "children" and not "things" or "objects," as St. Gregory of Nazianzus says, addressing Christ with this prayer: "Were it not for You, O my Christ, I would feel like a finite creature. I was born and I feel myself dissolve. I eat, I sleep, I rest, and I walk, I fall ill and I recover. Longings and torments without number assail me, I enjoy the sun and how the earth bears fruit. Then, I die and my flesh turns to dust just like that of animals, who have not sinned. But what have I more than them? Nothing, if not God. Were it not for you, O Christ mine, I would feel myself a lost creature. O, our Jesus, guide us from the cross to the resurrection and teach us that evil shall not have the last word, but love, mercy and forgiveness. O Christ, help us to exclaim again: 'Yesterday I was crucified with Christ; today I am glorified with him. Yesterday I died with him, today I live with him. Yesterday I was buried with him, today I am raised with him.'"

Finally, all together, let us remember the sick, let us remember all those who have been abandoned under the weight of the cross, that they may find in the trial of the cross the strength of hope, of hope, in the resurrection and love of God.

—Way of the Cross at Rome's Colosseum on Good Friday, April 18, 2014

For further reflection: We are "children," not "things" or "objects."

Behold the Cross

Where did Francis's journey to Christ begin? It began with *the gaze of the crucified Jesus*. With letting Jesus look at us at the very moment that he gives his life for us and draws us to himself. Francis experienced this in a special way in the Church of San Damiano, as he prayed before the cross which I too will have an opportunity to venerate. On that cross, Jesus is depicted not as dead, but alive! Blood is flowing from his wounded hands, feet, and side, but that blood speaks of life. Jesus' eyes are not closed but open, wide open: he looks at us in a way that touches our hearts. The cross does not speak to us about defeat and failure. Paradoxically, it speaks to us about a death which is life, a death which gives life, for it speaks to us of love, the love of God incarnate, a love which does not die but triumphs over evil and death. When we let the crucified Jesus gaze upon us, we are re-created, we become "a new creation." Everything else starts with this: the experience of transforming grace, the experience of being loved for no merits of our own, in spite of our being sinners. That is why Saint Francis could say with Saint Paul: "Far be it for me to glory except in the cross of our Lord Jesus Christ" (Gal 6:14).

We turn to you, Francis, and we ask you: Teach us to remain before the cross, to let the crucified Christ gaze upon us, to let ourselves be forgiven and re-created by his love.

—Sermon at Assisi, October 4, 2013

In the autumn of 2013, Pope Francis held at Saint Peter's Square a vigil for peace in Syria and the Near East. It was the longest papal ceremony in recent history. The initiative gathered diverse groups, including Syrian Muslims. Related to this event are the following texts.

My Christian faith urges me to look to the cross. How I wish that all men and women of good will would look to the cross if only for a moment! There, we can see God's reply: violence is not answered with violence, death is not answered with the language of death. In the silence of the cross, the uproar of weapons ceases and the language of reconciliation, forgiveness, dialogue, and peace is spoken. This evening, I ask the Lord that we Christians, and our brothers and sisters of other religions, and every man and woman of good will, cry out forcefully: violence and war are never the way to peace! Let everyone be moved to look into the depths of his or her conscience and listen to that word which says: Leave behind the self-interest that hardens your heart, overcome the indifference that makes your heart insensitive toward others, conquer your deadly reasoning, and open yourself to dialogue and reconciliation. Look upon your brother's sorrow—I think of the children: look upon these... look at the sorrow of your brother, stay your hand and do not add to it, rebuild the harmony that has been shattered; and all this achieved not by conflict but by encounter! May the noise of weapons cease! War always marks the failure of peace, it is always a defeat for humanity. Let the words of Pope Paul VI resound again: "No more one against the other, no more, never!... War never again, never again war!"... Let us pray this evening for reconciliation and peace, let us work for reconciliation and peace, and let us all become, in every place, men and women of reconciliation and peace! So may it be.

—*Prayer for Peace in the Middle East, Saint Peter's Square, September 25, 2013*

Only by contemplating Christ's suffering humanity can we become, gentle, humble, and tender like him. There is no other way. Of course, we must make the effort to seek Jesus, to think about his passion, how much he suffered, to think of his submissive silence. This will be our effort. Then all the rest comes from him and he will supply anything that is missing. But you must do this: hide your life with Christ in God.

To be good Christians it is necessary always to contemplate Jesus' humanity and all suffering humanity. To bear witness? Contemplate Jesus. To forgive? Contemplate Jesus' suffering. Not to hate our neighbor? Contemplate Jesus' suffering. Not to gossip against our neighbor? Contemplate Jesus' suffering. There is no other way.

—Morning Homily, September 12, 2013

THE CROSS AS JESUS' THRONE

The quotation from Fyodor Dostoyevsky in the following text could be evidence that this portion of the encyclical Lumen Fidei *truly originated from Francis's pen. Pope Bergoglio, who earlier taught literature, is an admirer of Russian authors. The encyclical itself emerged out of retired Pope Benedict XVI's material that Francis enriched.*

The clearest proof of the reliability of Christ's love is to be found in his dying for our sake. If laying down one's life for one's friends is the greatest proof of love (cf. Jn 15:13), Jesus offered his own life for all, even for his enemies, to transform their hearts. This explains why the evangelists could see the hour of Christ's crucifixion as the culmination of the gaze of faith; in that hour the depth and breadth of God's love shone forth... In Dostoevsky's *The Idiot,* Prince Myshkin sees a painting by Hans Holbein the Younger depicting Christ dead in the tomb and says: "Looking at that painting might cause one to lose his faith." The painting is a gruesome portrayal of the destructive effects of death on Christ's body. Yet it is precisely in contemplating Jesus' death that faith grows stronger and receives a dazzling light; then it is revealed as faith in Christ's steadfast love for us, a love capable of embracing death to bring us salvation. This love, which did not recoil before death in order to show its depth, is something I can believe in. Christ's total self-gift overcomes every suspicion and enables me to entrust myself to him completely.

Christ's death discloses the utter reliability of God's love above all in the light of his resurrection. As the risen one, Christ is the trustworthy witness, deserving of faith (cf. Rev 1:5; Heb 2:17), and a solid support for our faith. "If Christ has not been raised, your faith is futile," says Saint Paul (1 Cor 15:17). Had the Father's love not caused Jesus to rise from the dead, had it not been able to restore his body to life, then it would not be a completely reliable love, capable of illuminating also the gloom of death . . . Precisely because Jesus is the Son, because he is absolutely grounded in the Father, he was able to conquer death and make the fullness of life shine forth.

—*Encyclical* Lumen Fidei, *16, 17*

The following text by Francis includes a quotation from his predecessor's last address to the College of Cardinals, immediately before his retirement in February 2013.

Jesus enters Jerusalem in order to die on the cross. And it is precisely here that his kingship shines forth in godly fashion: his royal throne is the wood of the Cross! It reminds me of what Benedict XVI said to the cardinals: You are princes, but of a king crucified. That is the throne of Jesus. Jesus takes it upon himself... Why the cross? Because Jesus takes upon himself the evil, the filth, the sin of the world, including the sin of all of us, and he cleanses it, he cleanses it with his blood, with the mercy and the love of God. Let us look around: how many wounds are inflicted upon humanity by evil! Wars, violence, economic conflicts that hit the weakest, greed for money that you can't take with you and have to leave. When we were small, our grandmother used to say: a shroud has no pocket. Love of power, corruption, divisions, crimes against human life and against creation! And—as each one of us knows and is aware— our personal sins: our failures in love and respect toward God, toward our neighbor, and toward the whole of creation. Jesus on the cross feels the whole weight of the evil, and with the force of God's love he conquers it, he defeats it with his resurrection. This is the good that Jesus does for us on the throne of the cross. Christ's cross embraced with love never leads to sadness, but to joy, to the joy of having been saved and of doing a little of what he did on the day of his death.

—Sermon for Palm Sunday, May 24, 2013

... He Descended into Hell

The Shroud of Turin shows the image of a tortured and crucified man. Considered to be the shroud of Jesus, it is preserved in the Cathedral of Turin and is only rarely shown in public. During Holy Week in 2013 the shroud went on display for the first time on Italian television. Pope Francis recorded a video message for the occasion.

Dear Brothers and Sisters,

I join all of you gathered before the Holy Shroud, and I thank the Lord who, through modern technology, offers us this possibility.

Even if it takes place in this way, we do not merely "look," but rather we venerate by a prayerful gaze. I would go further: we are in fact looked upon ourselves. This face has eyes that are closed, it is the face of one who is dead, and yet mysteriously he is watching us, and in silence he speaks to us.

How is this possible? How is it that the faithful, like you, pause before this icon of a man scourged and crucified? It is because the Man of the Shroud invites us to contemplate Jesus of Nazareth. This image, impressed upon the cloth, speaks to our heart and moves us to climb the hill of Calvary, to look upon the wood of the cross, and to immerse ourselves in the eloquent silence of love.

Let us therefore allow ourselves to be reached by this look, which is directed not to our eyes but to our heart. In silence, let us listen to what he has to say to us from beyond death itself. By means of the Holy Shroud, the unique and supreme Word of God comes to us: Love made man, incarnate in our history; the merciful love of God who has taken upon himself all the evil of the world to free us from its power

This disfigured face resembles all those faces of men and women marred by a life which does not respect their dignity, by war and violence which afflict the weakest... And yet, at the same time, the face in the shroud conveys a great peace. This tortured body expresses a sovereign majesty. It is as if it let a restrained but powerful energy within it shine through, as if to say: Have faith, do not lose hope; the power of the love of God, the power of the Risen One overcomes all things.

So, looking upon the Man of the Shroud, I make my own the prayer that Saint Francis of Assisi prayed before the crucifix:

Most High, glorious God, enlighten the shadows of my heart, and grant me a right faith, a certain hope, and perfect charity, sense, and understanding, Lord, so that I may accomplish your holy and true command.

Amen.

—Message for the broadcast video of the Shroud of Turin, March 30, 2013

...On the Third Day He Rose Again from the Dead

Truly Raised Up

There are so many Christians without resurrection in the world today. Jesus is the one who conquers, he's the risen one. But often we don't feel it, we don't hear it well, although Jesus' resurrection is the very key to our faith. There are so many Christians without the risen Christ, those who stay with Jesus up to the tomb, weep, and care so much for him, but who aren't able to go any further.

The first of these are those on the morning of the resurrection, those on the road to Emmaus, who leave the city because they are afraid...The fearful are like that: they're afraid to think of the resurrection. And even the apostles, when Jesus appeared to them in the upper room, were frightened, fearing that they'd seen a ghost...Then there are the ashamed. Confessing that Christ is risen makes them feel rather embarrassed in this world that's so advanced in the sciences. Finally there are the triumphalist Christians who don't believe in the risen Christ and want to make for themselves a nobler resurrection than that of Jesus. They are "triumphalist," because they have an inferiority complex and adopt triumphalist attitudes in their lives, in their speeches, in their pastoral work and liturgy.

We need to recover the awareness that Jesus is risen. And to do so, Christians are called upon to gaze without fear, and without triumphalism, at his beauty, to put their fingers into his wounds and their hand into the side of Christ who is all in all, the fullness: Christ who is the center, Christ who is the hope, because he is the bridegroom and the conqueror. And he is a conqueror who re-creates the whole of creation.

—Morning Homily, September 10, 2013

☩ *For further reflection: Does belief in Jesus' resurrection influence my life?*

In the Creed we repeat these words: "and rose again on the third day in accordance with the scriptures." This is the very event that we are celebrating: the resurrection of Jesus, the center of the Christian message which has echoed from the beginning and was passed on so that it would come down to us. Saint Paul wrote to the Christians of Corinth: "I delivered to you as of first importance what I also received, that Christ died for our sins in accordance with the scriptures, that he was buried, that he was raised on the third day in accordance with the scriptures and that he appeared to Cephas, then to the Twelve" (1 Cor 15:3–5).

This brief profession of faith proclaims the Paschal Mystery itself with the first appearances of the Risen One to Peter and the Twelve: *the death and Resurrection of Jesus are the very heart of our hope*. Without this faith in the death and resurrection of Jesus our hope would be weak—but it would not even be hope. More precisely, the death and resurrection of Jesus are the heart of our hope. The apostle said: "If Christ has not been raised, your faith is futile and you are still in your sins" (v. 17).

Unfortunately, efforts have often been made to blur faith in the resurrection of Jesus and doubts have crept in, even among believers. It is a little like that "rosewater" faith, as we say; it is not a strong faith. And this is due to superficiality and sometimes to indifference, busy as we are with a thousand things considered more important than faith, or because we have a view of life that is solely horizontal.

However, it is the resurrection itself that opens us to greater hope, for it opens our life and the life of the world to the eternal future of God, to full happiness, to the certainty that evil, sin, and death may be overcome. And this leads to living daily situations with greater trust, to facing them with courage and determination. Christ's resurrection illuminates these everyday situations with a new light. The resurrection of Christ is our strength!

—General Audience, April 3, 2013

During his first trip to the Holy Land, Pope Francis met in Jerusalem's Basilica of the Holy Sepulcher with the leader of Orthodox Christians around the world, Ecumenical Patriarch Bartholomew I of Constantinople. The pope connected the mystery of the resurrection with the cause of Christian unity.

It is an extraordinary grace to be gathered here in prayer. The empty tomb, that new garden grave where Joseph of Arimathea reverently placed Jesus' body, is the place from which the proclamation of the resurrection begins: "Do not be afraid; I know that you are looking for Jesus who was crucified. He is not here, for he has been raised, as he said. Come, see the place where he lay. Then go quickly and tell his disciples, 'He has been raised from the dead'" (Mt 28:5–7). This proclamation, confirmed by the testimony of those to whom the risen Lord appeared, is the heart of the Christian message, faithfully passed down from generation to generation, as the apostle Paul, from the very beginning, bears witness: "I handed on to you as of first importance what I in turn had received: that Christ died for our sins in accordance with the scriptures, and that he was buried, and that he was raised on the third day in accordance with the scriptures" (1 Cor 15:3-4). This is the basis of the faith which unites us, whereby together we profess that Jesus Christ, the only-begotten Son of the Father and our sole Lord, "suffered under Pontius Pilate, was crucified, died and was buried; he descended into hell; on the third day he rose again from the dead" (Apostles' Creed). Each of us, everyone baptized in Christ, has spiritually risen from this tomb, for in baptism all of us truly became members of the body of the One who is the firstborn of all creation; we were buried together with him, so as to be raised up with him and to walk in newness of life (cf. Rom 6:4).

Let us receive the special grace of this moment. We pause in reverent silence before this empty tomb in order to rediscover the grandeur of our Christian vocation: we are men and women of resurrection, and not of death. From this place we learn how to live our lives, the trials of our churches and of the whole world, in the light of Easter morning. Every injury, every one of our pains and sorrows, has been borne on the shoulders of the Good Shepherd who offered himself in sacrifice and thereby opened the way to eternal life. His open wounds are like the cleft through which the torrent of his mercy is poured out upon the world... Let us not deprive the world of the joyful message of the resurrection! And let us not be deaf to the powerful summons to unity which rings out from this very place, in the words of the One who, risen from the dead, calls all of us "my brothers" (cf. Mt 28:10; Jn 20:17)...

Every time we ask forgiveness of one another for our sins against other Christians and every time we find the courage to grant and receive such forgiveness, we experience the resurrection! Every time we put behind us our longstanding prejudices and find the courage to build new fraternal relationships, we confess that Christ is truly risen! Every time we reflect on the future of the Church in the light of her vocation to unity, the dawn of Easter breaks forth!

—Address at the Basilica of the Holy Sepulcher, Jerusalem, May 25, 2014

We Believe in the Witness of the Women

It is striking how often Pope Francis stresses that the first witnesses to Jesus' resurrection were women. Their witness is for him a special sign of the reality of Jesus' resurrection.

How was the truth of faith in Christ's resurrection passed down to us? There are two kinds of testimony in the New Testament: some are in the form of a profession of faith, that is, of concise formulas that indicate the center of faith; while others are in the form of an account of the event of the resurrection and of the facts connected with it.

The former, in the form of a profession of faith, for example, is that of the letter to the Romans in which Saint Paul wrote: "If you confess with your lips that 'Jesus is Lord!' and believe in your heart that God raised him from the dead, you will be saved" (10:9). From the Church's very first steps faith in the mystery of the death and resurrection of Christ is firm and clear. Today, however, I would like to reflect on the latter, on the testimonies in the form of a narrative which we find in the gospels. First of all let us note that the first witnesses of this event were the women. At dawn they went to the tomb to anoint Jesus' body and found the first sign: the empty tomb (cf. Mk 16:1). Their meeting with a messenger of God followed. He announced: "Jesus of Nazareth, the Crucified One, has risen, he is not here" (cf. vv. 5–6). The women were motivated by love and were able to accept this announcement with faith: they believed and passed it on straight away, they did not keep it to themselves but passed it on.

They could not contain their joy in knowing that Jesus was alive, or the hope that filled their hearts. This should happen in our lives too. Let us feel the joy of being Christian! We believe in the Risen One who conquered evil and death! Let us have the courage to "come out of ourselves," to take this joy and this light to all the places of our life! The resurrection of Christ is our greatest certainty; he is our most precious treasure! How can we not share this treasure, this certainty, with others? It is not only for us, it is to be passed on, to be shared with others. Our testimony is precisely this.

Another point: in the profession of faith in the New Testament only men are recorded as witnesses of the resurrection, the apostles, but not the women. This is because, according to the Judaic law of that time, women and children could not bear trustworthy, credible witness. Instead in the gospels women play a fundamental lead role. Here we can grasp an element in favor of the historicity of the resurrection: if it was an invented event, in the context of that time it would not have been linked with the evidence of women. Instead the Evangelists simply recounted what happened: women were the first witnesses. This implies that God does not choose in accordance with human criteria: the first witnesses of the birth of Jesus were shepherds, simple, humble people; the first witnesses of the resurrection were women.

—General Audience, April 3, 2013

The apostles and disciples find it harder to believe. The women, not so. Peter runs to the tomb but stops at the empty tomb; Thomas has to touch the wounds on Jesus' body with his hands. On our way of faith it is also important to know and to feel that God loves us and not to be afraid to love him. Faith is professed with the lips and with the heart, with words and with love.

After his appearances to the women, others follow. Jesus makes himself present in a new way, he is the Crucified One but his body is glorified; he did not return to earthly life but returned in a new condition. At first they do not recognize him and it is only through his words and gestures that their eyes are opened. The meeting with the Risen One transforms, it gives faith fresh strength and a steadfast foundation. For us too there are many signs through which the Risen One makes himself known: sacred scripture, the Eucharist, the other sacraments, charity, all those acts of love which bring a ray of the Risen One. Let us permit ourselves to be illuminated by Christ's resurrection, let him transform us with his power, so that through us too the signs of death may give way to signs of life in the world.

—General Audience, April 3, 2013

The gospel of the resurrection of Jesus Christ begins with the journey of the women to the tomb at dawn on the day after the Sabbath. They go to the tomb to honor the body of the Lord, but they find it open and empty. A mighty angel says to them: "Do not be afraid!" (Mt 28:5) and orders them to go and tell the disciples: "He has been raised from the dead, and indeed he is going ahead of you to Galilee" (v. 7). The women quickly depart and on the way Jesus himself meets them and says: "Do not fear; go and tell my brothers to go to Galilee; there they will see me" (v. 10)...

Galilee is *the place where they were first called, where everything began!* To return there, to return to the place where they were originally called... to return to Galilee means *to re-read* everything on the basis of the cross and its victory, fearlessly: "Do not be afraid." To re-read everything—Jesus' preaching, his miracles, the new community, the excitement and the defections, even the betrayal—to re-read everything starting from the end, which is a new beginning, *from this supreme act of love...*

Where is my Galilee? Do I remember it? Have I forgotten it? Seek and you will find it! There the Lord is waiting for you. Have I gone off on roads and paths which made me forget it? Lord, help me: tell me what my Galilee is; for you know that I want to return there to encounter you and to let myself be embraced by your mercy. Do not be afraid, do not fear, return to Galilee!

The gospel is very clear: we need to go back there, to see Jesus risen, and to become witnesses of his resurrection. This is not to go back in time; it is not a kind of nostalgia. It is returning to our first love, in order to *receive the fire* which Jesus has kindled in the world and to bring that fire to all people, to the very ends of the earth. Go back to Galilee, without fear!

"Galilee of the Gentiles" (Mt 4:15; Is 8:23)! Horizon of the Risen Lord, horizon of the Church; intense desire of encounter... Let us be on our way!

—Sermon for the Easter Vigil, April 19, 2014

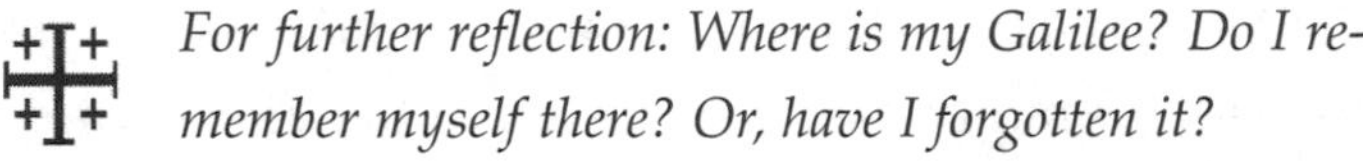

For further reflection: Where is my Galilee? Do I remember myself there? Or, have I forgotten it?

In the gospel of this radiant night of the Easter Vigil, we first meet the women who go the tomb of Jesus with spices to anoint his body... But at this point, something completely new and unexpected happens, something that upsets their hearts and their plans, something that will upset their whole life: they see the stone removed from before the tomb, they draw near and they do not find the Lord's body. It is an event that leaves them perplexed, hesitant, full of questions: "What happened?" "What is the meaning of all this?" (cf. Lk 24:4). Doesn't the same thing also happen to us when something completely new occurs in our everyday life? We stop short, we don't understand, we don't know what to do. *Newness* often makes us fearful, including the newness which God brings us, the newness which God asks of us. We are like the apostles in the gospel: often we would prefer to hold on to our own security, to stand in front of a tomb, to think about someone who has died, someone who ultimately lives on only as a memory, like the great historical figures from the past. We are afraid of God's surprises. Dear brothers and sisters, we are afraid of God's surprises! He always surprises us! The Lord is like that.

Dear brothers and sisters, let us not be closed to the newness that God wants to bring into our lives! Are we often weary, disheartened, and sad? Do we feel weighed down by our sins? Do we think that we won't be able to cope? Let us not close our hearts, let us not lose confidence, let us never give up: there are no situations which God cannot change, there is no sin which he cannot forgive if only we open ourselves to him.

—*Sermon for the Easter Vigil, March 30, 2013*

Nothing remains as it was before, not only in the lives of those women, but also in our own lives and in the history of mankind. Jesus is not dead, he has risen, he is *alive*! He does not simply return to life; rather, he is life itself, because he is the Son of God, the living God (cf. Num 14:21–28; Deut 5:26; Josh 3:10). Jesus no longer belongs to the past, but lives in the present and is projected toward the future; Jesus is the everlasting "today" of God. This is how the newness of God appears to the women, the disciples, and all of us: as victory over sin, evil and death, over everything that crushes life and makes it seem less human. And this is a message meant for me and for you dear sister, for you dear brother. How often does Love have to tell us: Why do you look for the living among the dead? Our daily problems and worries can wrap us up in ourselves, in sadness and bitterness... and that is where death is. That is not the place to look for the One who is alive!

Let the risen Jesus enter your life, welcome him as a friend, with trust: he is life! If up till now you have kept him at a distance, step forward. He will receive you with open arms. If you have been indifferent, take a risk: you won't be disappointed. If following him seems difficult, don't be afraid, trust him, be confident that he is close to you, he is with you and he will give you the peace you are looking for and the strength to live as he would have you do.

—Sermon for the Easter Vigil, March 30, 2013

The women encounter the newness of God. Jesus has risen, he is alive! But faced with empty tomb and the two men in brilliant clothes, their first reaction is one of fear: "They were terrified and bowed their faces to the ground." Saint Luke tells us that they didn't even have courage to look. But when they hear the message of the resurrection, they accept it in faith. And the two men in dazzling clothes tell them something of crucial importance: remember. "Remember what he told you when he was still in Galilee... And they remembered his words" (Lk 24:6, 8). This is the invitation to *remember* their encounter with Jesus, to remember his words, his actions, his life. And it is precisely this loving remembrance of their experience with the Master that enables the women to master their fear and to bring the message of the resurrection to the apostles and all the others (cf. Lk 24:9). To remember what God has done and continues to do for me, for us, to remember the road we have traveled; this is what opens our hearts to hope for the future. May we learn to remember everything that God has done in our lives.

—Sermon for the Easter Vigil, March 30, 2013

...He Ascended into Heaven

Let us remember first of all that in the ascension the Son of God brought to the Father our humanity, which he had taken on, and that he wants to draw all to himself, to call the whole world to be welcomed in God's embrace so that at the end of history the whole of reality may be consigned to the Father. Yet there is this "immediate time" between the first and the final coming of Christ, and that is the very time in which we are living.

—General Audience, April 24, 2013

The Upper Room reminds us of the Teacher's *farewell* and his *promise* to return to his friends: "When I go...I will come again and will take you to myself, that where I am you may be also" (Jn 14:3). Jesus does not leave us, nor does he ever abandon us; he precedes us to the house of the Father, where he desires to bring us as well.

—Sermon in the Upper Room, Jerusalem, May 26, 2014

The Acts of the Apostles recounts this episode, the final separation of the Lord Jesus from his disciples and from this world (cf. Acts 1:2–9). The gospel of Matthew, however, reports Jesus' mandate to his disciples: the invitation to go out, to set out in order to proclaim to all nations his message of salvation (cf. Mt 28:16–20). To "go" or, better, "depart" becomes the key word of today's feast: Jesus *departs* to the Father and commands his disciples to *depart* for the world.

Jesus *departs*, he ascends to heaven, that is, he returns to the Father from whom he had been sent to the world. He has finished his work, thus, he returns to the Father. But this does not mean a separation, for he remains forever with us, in a new way. By his ascension, the Risen Lord draws the gaze of the apostles—and our gaze—to the heights of heaven to show us that the end of our journey is the Father. He himself said that he would go to prepare a place for us in heaven. Yet, Jesus remains present and active in the affairs of human history through the power and the gifts of his Spirit; he is beside each of us. Even if we do not see him with our eyes, he is there! He accompanies us, he guides us, he takes us by the hand and he lifts us up when we fall down...

When Jesus returns to heaven, he brings the Father a gift. What is the gift? His wounds. His body is very beautiful, no bruises, no cuts from the scourging, but he retains his wounds. When he returns to the Father he shows him the wounds and says: "Behold Father, this is the price of the pardon you have granted." When the Father beholds the wounds of Jesus he forgives us forever, not because we are good, but because Jesus paid for us. Beholding the wounds of Jesus, the Father becomes most merciful.

This is the great work of Jesus today in heaven: showing the Father the price of forgiveness, his wounds. This is the beauty that urges us not to be afraid to ask forgiveness; the Father always pardons, because he sees the wounds of Jesus, he sees our sin and he forgives it.

But Jesus is present also through the Church, which he sent to extend his mission. Jesus' last message to his disciples is the mandate to *depart*: "Go therefore and make disciples of all nations" (Mt 28:19). It is a clear mandate, not just an option! The Christian community is a community "going forth." "In departure." More so: the Church was born "going forth." . . . To his missionary disciples Jesus says: "I am with you always, to the close of the age" (v. 20). Alone, without Jesus, we can do nothing! In apostolic work our own strengths, our resources, our structures do not suffice, even if they are necessary. Without the presence of the Lord and the power of his Spirit, our work, though it may be well organized, winds up being ineffective. And thus, we go to tell the nations who Jesus is.

— Angelus Prayer, Solemnity of the Ascension, June 1, 2014

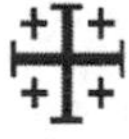

For further reflection: according to Francis, Jesus' fundamental change is our fundamental change.

Jesus has gone to the Father and from there he still intercedes, every day, at all times for us. And this is something current: Jesus before the Father, who offers his life, redemption, showing the Father his wounds, the price of salvation. And like this, every day Jesus interceded. This is why when we, for one reason or another, are a little down, let's remember that it is he who prays for us, who intercedes for us continuously. However, we often forget this. But Jesus did not go to heaven and send us the Holy Spirit, end of story! No! Presently, every moment, Jesus intercedes for us. May we pray with these simple words: "Lord Jesus, have mercy on me. Intercede for me."

—Morning Homily, January 22, 2015

. . . And Is Seated at the Right Hand of God the Father Almighty; From There He Will Come to Judge the Living and the Dead

He Will Truly Come Again

Mary teaches us to seize the right moment when Jesus comes into our life and asks for a ready and generous answer. And Jesus is coming. Indeed, the mystery of the birth of Jesus in Bethlehem took place historically more than two thousand years ago but occurs as a spiritual event in the "today" of the liturgy. The Word, who found a home in the virgin womb of Mary, comes in the celebration of Christmas to knock once again at the heart of every Christian. He comes and knocks. Each of us is called to respond, like Mary, with a personal and sincere "yes," placing ourselves fully at the disposal of God and of his mercy, of his love. How many times Jesus comes into our lives, and how many times he sends us an angel, and how many times we don't notice because we are so taken, immersed in our own thoughts, in our own affairs, and even, in these days, in our Christmas preparations, so as not to notice him who comes and knocks at the door of our hearts, asking for acceptance, asking for a "yes" like Mary's.

—Angelus Prayer, December 21, 2014

 *For further reflection: Do I await him?*

A heart that loves the law, for the law is God's, but that also loves God's surprises, for his "holy law is not an end in itself": this is a journey, a teaching that leads us to Jesus Christ. In today's gospel (Lk 11:29–32), Jesus harshly criticizes the crowd gathered to hear him, as "an evil generation" because "it seeks a sign." It is evident that Jesus is speaking to the doctors of the law who, many times in the gospel, ask him for a sign. Indeed, they do not see many of Jesus' signs. But this is precisely why Jesus scolds them on various occasions: "You are incapable of seeing the signs of the times," he tells them in the gospel of Matthew, drawing upon the image of the fig tree: "As soon as its branch becomes tender and puts forth its leaves, you know that summer is near; and you do not understand the signs of the times."

Why did the doctors of the law not understand the signs of the times and request an extraordinary sign? There are several answers. The first is because they were closed. They were closed within their system, they had organized the law very well. It was a masterpiece... But Jesus caught them unprepared, by doing curious things, such as associating with sinners and eating with the publicans. And the doctors of the law did not like this; they found it dangerous, putting at risk the doctrine that they, the theologians, had been fashioning for centuries. It was a law made for love, in order to be faithful to God, but it had become a closed regulatory system. They had simply forgotten history. They had forgotten that God is the God of the law, but he is also the God of surprises. And God had surprises in store for his people many times... Despite that, however, they did not understand that God is always new; he never denies himself, he never says that what he had said was a mistake, never; but he always surprises. And they did not understand and they closed themselves within that system created with much good will; and they asked that Jesus give them a sign, failing to understand, however, the many signs that Jesus had given and maintaining a completely closed attitude.

The second reason is attributable to the fact that they had forgotten that they were a people on a journey. And when one is on a journey he always finds new things, things he does not know. And in the law, they had to accept these things in a heart faithful to the Lord. But, also in this case, a journey is not absolute in itself, it is a journey toward an end point: toward the definitive manifestation of the Lord. After all, all of life is a journey toward the fullness of Jesus Christ, when the second coming occurs. It is a journey toward Jesus, who will come again in glory, as the angels said to the apostles on the day of the ascension. In other words, this generation seeks a sign, but no sign shall bc given to it except the sign of Jonah: in other words, the sign of the resurrection, of glory, of that eschatology toward which we are journeying. However, many of his contemporaries were closed within themselves, not open to the God of surprises; they were men and women who did not know the path or even this eschatology.

We must ask ourselves: Am I attached to my things, to my ideas, am I closed? Or am I open to the God of surprises? Am I a stationary person or a person on a journey? And finally, do I believe in Jesus Christ and in what he has done? That is, that he died and rose again... Do I believe that the journey goes forth toward maturity, toward the manifestation of the glory of the Lord? Am I capable of understanding the signs of the times and of being faithful to the voice of the Lord that is manifest in them?

—*Morning Homily, October 13, 2014*

We Live In the In-Between Time

In the Creed we profess that Jesus "will come again in glory to judge the living and the dead." Human history begins with the creation of man and woman in God's likeness and ends with the last judgment of Christ. These two poles of history are often forgotten; and, at times, especially faith in Christ's return and in the last judgment is not so clear and firm in Christian hearts. In his public life Jesus frequently reflected on the reality of his final coming.

—General Audience, April 24, 2013

Let us remember first of all that in the ascension the Son of God brought to the Father our humanity, which he had taken on, and that he wants to draw all to himself, to call the whole world to be welcomed in God's embrace so that at the end of history the whole of reality may be consigned to the Father. Yet there is this "immediate time" between the first and the final coming of Christ, and that is the very time in which we are living. The parable of the ten virgins fits into this context of "immediate" time (cf. Mt 25:1–13). They are ten maidens who are awaiting the arrival of the bridegroom, but he is late and they fall asleep. At the sudden announcement that the bridegroom is arriving they prepare to welcome him, but while five of them, who are wise, have oil to burn in their lamps, the others, who are foolish, are left with lamps that have gone out because they have no oil for them. While they go to get some oil the bridegroom arrives and the foolish virgins find that the door to the hall of the marriage feast is shut.

They knock on it again and again, but it is now too late, the bridegroom answers: I do not know you. The bridegroom is the Lord, and the time of waiting for his arrival is the time he gives to us, to all of us, before his final coming with mercy and patience; it is a time of watchfulness, a time in which we must keep alight the lamps of faith, hope, and charity, a time in which to keep our heart open to goodness, beauty, and truth. It is a time to live in accordance with God, because we do not know either the day or the hour of Christ's return. What he asks of us is to be ready for the encounter—ready for an encounter, for a beautiful encounter, the encounter with Jesus, which means being able to see the signs of his presence, keeping our faith alive with prayer, with the sacraments, and taking care not to fall asleep so as to not forget about God. The life of slumbering Christians is a sad life, it is not a happy life. Christians must be happy, with the joy of Jesus. Let us not fall asleep!

—*General Audience, April 24, 2013*

The second parable, the parable of the talents, makes us think about the relationship between how we use the gifts we have received from God and his return, when he will ask us what use we made of them (cf. Mt 25:14–30). We are well acquainted with the parable: before his departure the master gives a few talents to each of his servants to ensure that they will be put to good use during his absence. He gives five to the first servant, two to the second one, and one to the third. In the period of their master's absence, the first two servants increase their talents—these are ancient coins—whereas the third servant prefers to bury his and to return it to his master as it was.

On his return, the master judges what they have done: he praises the first two while he throws the third one out into the outer darkness because, through fear, he had hidden his talent, withdrawing into himself. A Christian who withdraws into himself, who hides everything that the Lord has given him, is a Christian who . . . is not a Christian! He is a Christian who does not thank God for everything God has given him!

This tells us that the expectation of the Lord's return is the time of action—we are in the time of action—the time in which we should bring God's gifts to fruition, not for ourselves but for him, for the Church, for others, the time to seek to increase goodness in the world always, and in particular, in this period of crisis, today, it is important not to turn in on ourselves, burying our own talent, our spiritual, intellectual, and material riches, everything that the Lord has given us, but, rather to open ourselves, to be supportive, to be attentive to others.

—General Audience, April 24, 2013

Finally, a word about the passage on the last judgment in which the Lord's second coming is described, when he will judge all human beings, the living and the dead (cf. Mt 25: 31–46). The image used by the evangelist is that of the shepherd who separates the sheep from the goats. On his right he places those who have acted in accordance with God's will, who went to the aid of their hungry, thirsty, foreign, naked, sick or imprisoned neighbor—I said "foreign": I am thinking of the multitude of foreigners who are here in the diocese of Rome: What do we do for them? While on his left are those who did not help their neighbor. This tells us that God will judge us on our love, on how we have loved our brethren, especially the weakest and the neediest. Of course we must always have clearly in mind that we are justified, we are saved through grace, through an act of freely given love by God who always goes before us. On our own we can do nothing. Faith is first of all a gift we have received. But in order to bear fruit, God's grace always demands our openness to him, our free and tangible response. Christ comes to bring us the mercy of a God who saves. We are asked to trust in him, to respond to the gift of his love with a good life, made up of actions motivated by faith and love.

—General Audience, April 24, 2013

Questions Concerning the Last Judgment

Dear brothers and sisters, may looking at the last judgment never frighten us: rather, may it impel us to live the present better. God offers us this time with mercy and patience so that we may learn every day to recognize him in the poor and in the lowly. Let us strive for goodness and be watchful in prayer and in love. May the Lord, at the end of our life and at the end of history, be able to recognize us as good and faithful servants.

—*General Audience, April 24, 2013*

Look, read the beatitudes: that will do you good. If you want to know what you actually have to do, read Matthew chapter 25, which is the standard by which we will be judged. With these two things you have the action plan: the beatitudes and Matthew 25. You do not need to read anything else. I ask you this with all my heart.

—*Address to Argentinian youth in Rio de Janeiro, July 25, 2013*

The beatitudes are the portrait of Jesus, his way of life; and they are the path to true happiness, which we too can travel with the grace that Jesus gives us.

Besides the new law, Jesus also gives us the "protocol" by which we will be judged. At the end of the world we will be judged. And what questions will we be asked there? What will these questions be? What is the protocol by which the judge will evaluate us? We find it in chapter 25 of the gospel of Matthew. Today the assignment is to read the fifth chapter of the gospel of Matthew where the beatitudes are; and read the 25th chapter, where the protocol is, the questions that we will be asked on judgment day. We will not have titles, credit, or privileges on which to stake our claims. The Lord will recognize us if, in our turn, we recognized him in the poor, in the hungry, in the indigent and the outcast, in those who suffer and are alone... This is one of the fundamental criteria for evaluating our Christian life, which Jesus calls us to measure up to every day. I read the beatitudes and I think of how my Christian life should be, and then I examine my conscience with this chapter 25 of Matthew. Every day: I did this, I did this, I did this... It will do us good! They are simple but concrete things.

—General Audience, August 6, 2014

Christ Is the Center

Christian faith is centered on Christ; it is the confession that Jesus is Lord and that God has raised him from the dead (cf. Rom 10:9). All the threads of the Old Testament converge on Christ; he becomes the definitive "Yes" to all the promises, the ultimate basis of our "Amen" to God (cf. 2 Cor 1:20). The history of Jesus is the complete manifestation of God's reliability. If Israel continued to recall God's great acts of love, which formed the core of its confession of faith and broadened its gaze in faith, the life of Jesus now appears as the locus of God's definitive intervention, the supreme manifestation of his love for us. The word which

God speaks to us in Jesus is not simply one word among many, but his eternal Word (cf. Heb 1:1–2).

—*Encyclical* Lumen Fidei, *15*

Christ is at the center, Christ is the center. Christ is the center of creation, Christ is the center of his people and Christ is the center of history... In him, through him, and for him all things were created. He is the center of all things, he is the beginning: Jesus Christ, the Lord. God has given him the fullness, the totality, so that in him all things might be reconciled (cf. Col 1:12–20). He is the Lord of creation, he is the Lord of reconciliation...

And so the attitude demanded of us as true believers is that of recognizing and accepting in our lives the centrality of Jesus Christ, in our thoughts, in our words, and in our works. And so our thoughts will be *Christian* thoughts, thoughts of Christ. Our works will be *Christian* works, works of Christ; and our words will be *Christian* words, words of Christ. But when this center is lost, when it is replaced by something else, only harm can result for everything around us and for ourselves.

—*Sermon at the end of the Year of Faith, November 24, 2013*

Christ is *the center of the history of humanity and also the center of the history of every individual.* To him we can bring the joys and the hopes, the sorrows and troubles which are part of our lives. When Jesus is the center, light shines even amid the darkest times of our lives; he gives us hope, as he does to the good thief in today's gospel.

Whereas all the others treat Jesus with disdain—"If you are the Christ, the Messiah King, save yourself by coming down from the cross!"—the thief who went astray in his life but now repents clings to the crucified Jesus and begs him: "Remember me, when you come into your kingdom" (Lk 23:42). Jesus promises him: "Today you will be with me in paradise" (v. 43), in his kingdom. Jesus speaks only a word of forgiveness, not of condemnation. Whenever anyone finds the courage to ask for this forgiveness, the Lord does not let such a petition go unheard. Today we can all think of our own history, our own journey. Each of us has his or her own history: we think of our mistakes, our sins, our good times and our bleak times. We would do well, each one of us, on this day, to think about our own personal history, to look at Jesus and to keep telling him, sincerely and quietly: "Remember me, Lord, now that you are in your kingdom! Jesus, remember me, because I want to be good, but I just don't have the strength: I am a sinner, I am a sinner. But remember me, Jesus! You can remember me because you are at the center, you are truly in your kingdom!" How beautiful this is! Let us all do this today, each one of us in his or her own heart, again and again. "Remember me, Lord, you who are at the center, you who are in your kingdom."

Jesus' promise to the good thief gives us great hope. It tells us that God's grace is always greater than the prayer which sought it. The Lord always grants more; he is so generous, he always gives more than what he has been asked: you ask him to remember you, and he brings you into his kingdom!

Let us ask the Lord to remember us, in the certainty that by his mercy we will be able to share his glory in paradise. Let us go forward together on this road!

—Sermon at the end of the Year of Faith, November 24, 2013

For further reflection: Does Christ stand at the center for me? Or does something or someone else stand there?

✠

I Believe in the Holy Spirit

When Pope Francis speaks about the Holy Spirit, he relies not on definitions but on descriptive, dynamic forms of speech: The Spirit is "freshness, imagination, newness."

The Holy Spirit is the soul of the Church. He *gives life*, he *brings forth different charisms* which enrich the people of God and, above all, he *creates unity* among believers: from the many he makes one body, the Body of Christ. The Church's whole life and mission depend on the Holy Spirit; he fulfills all things . . . He is freshness, imagination, and newness.

—Sermon in Istanbul, Turkey, November 29, 2014

God's Life in Us

In the Creed we profess with faith: "I believe in the Holy Spirit, the Lord and Giver of life." The first truth to which we adhere in the Creed is that the Holy Spirit is *Kýrios*,

Lord. This signifies that he is truly God, just as the Father and the Son; the object, on our part, of the same act of adoration and glorification that we address to the Father and to the Son. Indeed, the Holy Spirit is the third person of the Most Holy Trinity; he is the great gift of Christ Risen who opens our mind and our heart to faith in Jesus as the Son sent by the Father and who leads us to friendship, to communion with God.

However, I would like to focus especially on the fact that *the Holy Spirit is the inexhaustible source of God's life in us*. Man of every time and place desires a full and beautiful life, just and good, a life that is not threatened by death, but can still mature and grow to fullness. Man is like a traveler who, crossing the deserts of life, thirsts for the living water: gushing and fresh, capable of quenching his deep desire for light, love, beauty, and peace. We all feel this desire! And Jesus gives us this living water: he is the Holy Spirit, who proceeds from the Father and whom Jesus pours out into our hearts. "I came that they may have life, and have it abundantly," Jesus tells us (Jn 10:10).

—General Audience, May 8, 2013

Jesus promised the Samaritan woman that he would give a superabundance of "living water" forever to all those who recognize him as the Son sent by the Father to save us (cf. Jn 4:5–26; 3:17). Jesus came to give us this "living water," who is the Holy Spirit, that our life might be guided by

God, might be moved by God, nourished by God. When we say that a Christian is a spiritual being we mean just this: the Christian is a person who thinks and acts in accordance with God, in accordance with the Holy Spirit. But I ask myself: And do we, do we think in accordance with God? Do we act in accordance with God? Or do we let ourselves be guided by the many other things that certainly do not come from God? Each one of us needs to respond to this in the depths of his or her own heart.

At this point we may ask ourselves: Why can this water quench our thirst deep down? We know that water is essential to life; without water we die; it quenches, washes, makes the earth fertile. In the letter to the Romans we find these words: "God's love has been poured into our hearts through the Holy Spirit who has been given to us" (5:5). The "living water," the Holy Spirit, is the gift of the Risen One who dwells in us, purifies us, illuminates us, renews us, transforms us because he makes us participants in the very life of God that is Love. That is why the apostle Paul says that the Christian's life is moved by the Holy Spirit and by his fruits, which are "love, joy, peace, patience, kindness, goodness, faithfulness, gentleness, self-control" (Gal 5:22–23). *The Holy Spirit introduces us to divine life as "children in the Only Begotten Son."*

In another passage from the letter to the Romans that we have recalled several times, Saint Paul sums it up with these words: "For all who are led by the Spirit of God are sons of God. For you . . . have received the spirit of sonship.

When we cry, '*Abba*! Father!' it is the Spirit himself bearing witness with our spirit that we are children of God, and if children, then heirs, heirs of God and fellow heirs with Christ, provided we suffer with him in order that we may also be glorified with him" (8:14–17). This is the precious gift that the Holy Spirit brings to our hearts: the very life of God, the life of true children, a relationship of confidence, freedom, and trust in the love and mercy of God. It also gives us a new perception of others, close and far, seen always as brothers and sisters in Jesus to be respected and loved.

—General Audience, May 8, 2013

The Holy Spirit teaches us to see with the eyes of Christ, to live life as Christ lived, to understand life as Christ understood it. That is why the living water, who is the Holy Spirit, quenches our life, why he tells us that we are loved by God as children, that we can love God as his children, and that by his grace we can live as children of God, like Jesus. And we, do we listen to the Holy Spirit? What does the Holy Spirit tell us? He says: God loves you. He tells us this. God loves you, God likes you. Do we truly love God and others as Jesus does? Let us allow ourselves to be guided by the Holy Spirit, let us allow him to speak to our heart and say this to us: God is love, God is waiting for us, God is Father, he loves us as a true father loves, he loves us truly and only the Holy Spirit can tell us this in our hearts.

Let us hear the Holy Spirit, let us listen to the Holy Spirit and may we move forward on this path of love, mercy, and forgiveness.

—General Audience, May 8, 2013

What Occurred at Pentecost

The evangelist brings us back to Jerusalem, to the upper room where the apostles were gathered. The first element that draws our attention is the sound which suddenly came from heaven "like the rush of a violent wind" and filled the house; then the "tongues as of fire" which divided and came to rest on each of the apostles. Sound and tongues of fire: these are clear, concrete signs that touch the apostles not only from without but also within: deep in their minds and hearts. As a result, "all of them were filled with the Holy Spirit," who unleashed his irresistible power with amazing consequences: they all "began to speak in different languages, as the Spirit gave them ability." A completely unexpected scene opens up before our eyes: a great crowd gathers, astonished because each one hears the apostles speaking in his own language. They all experience something new, something which has never happened before: "We hear them, each of us, speaking our own language." And what is it that they are they speaking about? "God's deeds of power."

—Sermon for Pentecost, May 19, 2013

Often we follow him, we accept him, but only up to a certain point. It is hard to abandon ourselves to him with complete trust, allowing the Holy Spirit to be the soul and guide of our lives in our every decision. We fear that God may force us to strike out on new paths and leave behind our all too narrow, closed, and selfish horizons in order to become open to his own. Yet throughout the history of salvation, whenever God reveals himself, he brings newness—God always brings newness—and demands our complete trust: Noah, mocked by all, builds an ark and is saved; Abram leaves his land with only a promise in hand; Moses stands up to the might of Pharaoh and leads his people to freedom; the apostles, huddled fearfully in the upper room, go forth with courage to proclaim the gospel. This is not a question of novelty for novelty's sake, the search for something new to relieve our boredom, as is so often the case in our own day. The newness which God brings into our life is something that actually brings fulfillment, that gives true joy, true serenity, because God loves us and desires only our good.

Let us ask ourselves today: Are we open to "God's surprises"? Or are we closed and fearful before the newness of the Holy Spirit? Do we have the courage to strike out along the new paths which God's newness sets before us, or do we resist, barricaded in transient structures which have lost their capacity for openness to what is new? We would do well to ask ourselves these questions all through the day.

—*Sermon for Pentecost, May 19, 2013*

The Holy Spirit would appear to create disorder in the Church, since he brings the diversity of charisms and gifts; yet all this, by his working, is a great source of wealth, for the Holy Spirit is the Spirit of unity, which does not mean uniformity, but which leads everything back to *harmony*. In the Church, it is the Holy Spirit who creates harmony. One of the fathers of the Church has an expression which I love: the Holy Spirit himself is harmony—*"Ipse harmonia est."* He is indeed harmony. Only the Spirit can awaken diversity, plurality, and multiplicity, while at the same time building unity. Here too, when we are the ones who try to create diversity and close ourselves up in what makes us different and other, we bring division. When we are the ones who want to build unity in accordance with our human plans, we end up creating uniformity, standardization. But if instead we let ourselves be guided by the Spirit, richness, variety, and diversity never become a source of conflict, because he impels us to experience variety within the communion of the Church. Journeying together in the Church, under the guidance of her pastors who possess a special charism and ministry, is a sign of the working of the Holy Spirit. Having a sense of the Church is something fundamental for every Christian, every community and every movement. It is the Church which brings Christ to me, and me to Christ; parallel journeys are very dangerous! When we venture beyond (*proagon*) the Church's teaching and community—the apostle John tells us in his second letter—

and do not remain in them, we are not one with the God of Jesus Christ (cf. 2 Jn v. 9). So let us ask ourselves: Am I open to the harmony of the Holy Spirit, overcoming every form of exclusivity? Do I let myself be guided by him, living in the Church and with the Church?

—*Sermon for Pentecost, May 19, 2013*

The older theologians used to say that the soul is a kind of sailboat, the Holy Spirit is the wind which fills its sails and drives it forward, and the gusts of wind are the gifts of the Spirit. Lacking his impulse and his grace, we do not go forward. The Holy Spirit draws us into the mystery of the living God and saves us from the threat of a Church which is gnostic and self-referential, closed in on herself; he impels us to open the doors and go forth to proclaim and bear witness to the good news of the gospel, to communicate the joy of faith, the encounter with Christ. The Holy Spirit is the soul of *mission*. The events that took place in Jerusalem almost two thousand years ago are not something far removed from us; they are events which affect us and become a lived experience in each of us. The Pentecost of the upper room in Jerusalem is the beginning, a beginning which endures.

The Holy Spirit is the supreme gift of the risen Christ to his apostles, yet he wants that gift to reach everyone. As we heard in the gospel, Jesus says: "I will ask the Father, and he will give you another advocate to remain with you forever"

(Jn 14:16). It is the Paraclete Spirit, the "Comforter," who grants us the courage to take to the streets of the world, bringing the gospel! The Holy Spirit makes us look to the horizon and drive us to the very outskirts of existence in order to proclaim life in Jesus Christ. Let us ask ourselves: do we tend to stay closed in on ourselves, on our group, or do we let the Holy Spirit open us to mission?

—Sermon for Pentecost, May 19, 2013

Speaking to the apostles at the Last Supper, Jesus said that after he left this world he would send them *the gift of the Father*, that is, the Holy Spirit (cf. Jn 15:26). This promise was powerfully fulfilled on the day of Pentecost, when the Holy Spirit descended upon the disciples who were gathered in the upper room. This extraordinary outpouring was not limited solely to that moment, but was an event that was renewed and still continues to be renewed. Christ glorified at the right hand of the Father continues to fulfill his promise, sending upon the Church the life-giving Spirit, who *teaches* us, *reminds* us, and *lets* us *speak*.

The Holy Spirit *teaches us*: he is the Interior Master. He guides us along the right path, through life's challenges. He teaches us the path, the way. In the early times of the Church, Christianity was called "the way" (cf. Acts 9:2), and Jesus himself is the Way. The Holy Spirit teaches us to follow him, to walk in his footprints. More than a master of doctrine, the Holy Spirit is a master of life. And he surely takes part in life as well as in knowledge, but within the broadest and most harmonious horizons of Christian existence.

—*Sermon for Pentecost, June 8, 2014*

The Work of the Holy Spirit

When we welcome the Holy Spirit into our hearts and allow him to act, Christ makes himself present in us and takes shape in our lives; through us, it will be he—Christ himself—who prays, forgives, gives hope and consolation, serves the brethren, draws close to the needy and to the least, creates community, and sows peace. Think how important this is: by means of the Holy Spirit, Christ himself comes to do all this among us and for us. That is why it is important that children and young people receive the sacrament of confirmation.

—*General Audience, January 29, 2014*

Jesus himself told his disciples: the Holy Spirit "will guide you into all the truth" (Jn 16:13), since he himself is "the Spirit of Truth" (cf. Jn 14:17; 15:26; 16:13). We are living in an age in which people are rather skeptical of truth. Benedict XVI has frequently spoken of relativism, that is, of the tendency to consider nothing definitive and to think that truth comes from consensus or from something we like. The question arises: Does "the" truth really exist?

What is "the" truth? Can we know it? Can we find it? Here springs to my mind the question of Pontius Pilate, the Roman procurator, when Jesus reveals to him the deep meaning of his mission: "What is truth?" (Jn 18:37, 38). Pilate cannot understand that "the" Truth is standing in front of him, he cannot see in Jesus the face of the truth that is the face of God. And yet Jesus is exactly this: the Truth that, in the fullness of time, "became flesh" (cf. Jn 1:1, 14), and came to dwell among us so that we might know it. The truth is not grasped as a thing, the truth is encountered. It is not a possession, it is an encounter with a Person.

But who can enable us to recognize that Jesus is "the" Word of truth, the Only-Begotten Son of God the Father? Saint Paul teaches that "no one can say 'Jesus is Lord' except by the Holy Spirit" (1 Cor 12:3). It is the Holy Spirit himself, the gift of the Risen Christ, who makes us recognize the Truth. Jesus describes him as the "Paraclete," namely, "the one who comes to our aid," who is beside us to sustain us on this journey of knowledge; and, at the Last Supper, Jesus assures the disciples that the Holy Spirit will teach them all things and remind them of all he has said to them (cf. Jn 14:26).

So how does the Holy Spirit act in our life and in the life of the Church in order to guide us to the truth? First of all he recalls and impresses in the heart of believers the words Jesus spoke and, through these very words, the law of God—as the prophets of the Old Testament had foretold—

is engraved in our heart and becomes within us a criterion for evaluation in decisions and for guidance in our daily actions; it becomes a principle to live by.

—General Audience, May 15, 2013

Let us try asking ourselves: am I open to the action of the Holy Spirit? Do I pray him to give me illumination, to make me more sensitive to God's things? This is a prayer we must pray every day: "Holy Spirit, make my heart open to the word of God, make my heart open to goodness, make my heart open to the beauty of God every day." I would like to ask everyone a question: How many of you pray every day to the Holy Spirit? There will not be many but we must fulfill Jesus' wish and pray every day to the Holy Spirit that he open our heart to Jesus.

Let us think of Mary who "kept all these things, pondering them in her heart" (Lk 2:19, 51). Acceptance of the words and truth of faith so that they may become life is brought about and increases under the action of the Holy Spirit. In this regard we must learn from Mary, we must relive her "yes," her unreserved readiness to receive the Son of God in her life, which was transformed from that moment. Through the Holy Spirit, the Father and the Son take up their abode with us: we live in God and of God.

—General Audience, May 15, 2013

Through the Holy Spirit, the Father and the Son take up their abode with us: we live in God and of God. Yet is our life truly inspired by God? How many things do I put before God?

Dear brothers and sisters, we need to let ourselves be bathed in the light of the Holy Spirit so that he may lead us into the truth of God, who is the one Lord of our life. In this Year of Faith let us ask ourselves whether we really have taken some steps to know Christ and the truth of faith better by reading and meditating on sacred scripture, by studying the Catechism, and by receiving the sacraments regularly. However, let us ask ourselves at the same time what steps we are taking to ensure that faith governs the whole of our existence.

We are not Christian "part-time," only at certain moments, in certain circumstances, in certain decisions; no one can be Christian in this way. We are Christian all the time! Totally! May Christ's truth, which the Holy Spirit teaches us and gives to us, always and totally affect our daily life. Let us call on him more often so that he may guide us on the path of disciples of Christ. Let us call on him every day. I am making this suggestion to you: let us invoke the Holy Spirit every day. In this way the Holy Spirit will bring us close to Jesus Christ.

—General Audience, May 15, 2013

For further reflection: Am I a Christian at all times or only part time?

Concerning the Holy Spirit in the Holy Land

We are not far from where the Holy Spirit descended with power on Jesus of Nazareth after his baptism by John in the River Jordan (cf. Mt 3:16) and today I will go there. Today's gospel, and this place to which, by God's grace, I have come as a pilgrim, invite us to meditate on the Holy Spirit and on all that he has brought about in Christ and in us. In a word, we can say that the Holy Spirit carries out three actions—he *prepares*, he *anoints*, and he *sends*.

At the baptism, the Holy Spirit descended upon Jesus to *prepare* him for his mission of salvation, the mission of one who is a servant, humble and meek, ready to share and give himself completely. Yet the Holy Spirit, present from the beginning of salvation history, had already been at work in Jesus from the moment of his conception in the virginal womb of Mary of Nazareth, by bringing about the wondrous event of the Incarnation: "The Holy Spirit will come upon you, will overshadow you," the Angel said to Mary, "and you will give birth to a son who will be named Jesus" (cf. Lk 1:35). The Holy Spirit had then acted in Simeon and Anna on the day of the presentation of Jesus in the temple (cf. Lk 2:22). Both were awaiting the Messiah, and both were inspired by the Holy Spirit. Simeon and Anna, upon seeing the child, knew immediately that he was the one long awaited by the people. They gave prophetic expression to the joy of encountering the redeemer and, in a certain sense, served as a *preparation* for the encounter between the Messiah and the people.

These various works of the Holy Spirit are part of a harmonious action, a sole divine plan of love. The mission of the Holy Spirit, in fact, is *to beget harmony*—he is himself harmony—and *to create peace* in different situations and between different people. Diversity of ideas and persons should not trigger rejection or prove an obstacle, for variety always enriches. So today, with fervent hearts, we invoke the Holy Spirit and ask him *to prepare* the path to peace and unity.

The Holy Spirit also *anoints*. He anointed Jesus inwardly and he anoints his disciples, so that they can have the mind of Christ and thus be disposed to live lives of peace and communion. Through the anointing of the Spirit, our human nature is sealed with the holiness of Jesus Christ and we are enabled to love our brothers and sisters with the same love that God has for us. We ought, therefore, to show concrete signs of humility, fraternity, forgiveness, and reconciliation. These signs are the prerequisite of a true, stable, and lasting peace. Let us ask the Father to anoint us so that we may fully become his children, ever more conformed to Christ, and may learn to see one another as brothers and sisters. Thus, by putting aside our grievances and divisions, we can show fraternal love for one another. This is what Jesus asks of us in the gospel: "If you love me, you will keep my commandments. And I will pray the Father, and he will give you another Paraclete, to be with you forever" (Jn 14:15–16).

Lastly, the Holy Spirit *sends*. Jesus is the one who is sent forth, filled with the Spirit of the Father. Anointed by the same Spirit, we also are *sent* as messengers and witnesses of peace. The world has much need of us as messengers of peace, witnesses of peace! The world needs this. The world asks us to bring peace and to be a sign of peace!...

Dear friends! Dear brothers and sisters! The Holy Spirit descended upon Jesus in the Jordan and thus inaugurated his work of redemption to free the world from sin and death. Let us ask the Spirit *to prepare* our hearts to encounter our brothers and sisters, so that we may overcome our differences rooted in political thinking, language, culture, and religion. Let us ask him *to anoint* our whole being with the oil of his mercy, which heals the injuries caused by mistakes, misunderstandings and disputes. And let us ask him for the grace *to send* us forth, in humility and meekness, along the demanding but enriching path of seeking peace.

—Sermon in Amman, Jordan on May 24, 2014

...The Holy Catholic Church

On no other article of the Apostles' Creed are there so many statements by Pope Francis than on the theme of the Church. These occur above all because for many months he devoted his general audience on Wednesdays to catechesis. In response to a journalist who tried to trip him up somewhat during a press conference, the pope said, "I am a son of the Church!" (return flight from Rio to Rome on July 28, 2013).

Here, where Jesus shared the Last Supper with the apostles; where, after his resurrection, he appeared in their midst; where the Holy Spirit descended with power upon Mary and the disciples, here the Church was born, and she was born *to go forth*. From here she *set out*, with the broken bread in her hands, the wounds of Christ before her eyes, and the Spirit of love in her heart...

The upper room reminds us of the birth of the *new family*, the Church, our holy Mother the hierarchical Church established by the risen Jesus...

These horizons are opened up by the upper room, the horizons of the Risen Lord and his Church. From here the Church goes forth, impelled by the life-giving breath of the Spirit. Gathered in prayer with the Mother of Jesus, the Church lives in constant expectation of a renewed outpouring of the Holy Spirit. Send forth your Spirit, Lord, and renew the face of the earth (cf. Ps 104:30)!

—Sermon in Jerusalem, May 26, 2014

The four quotations that follow are selections from the pope's catechesis on the theme of the Church during his general audiences on Wednesdays in Rome.

Our Mother, Our Family

Today I begin a new series of catecheses on the Church. It is a little like a child speaking of his own mother, his family. To speak of the Church is to speak of our mother, of our family. The Church, in fact, is not an institution focused in on itself or a private association, an NGO, and even less should it restrict its gaze to the clergy or to the Vatican.

"The Church thinks..." But the Church is all of us! "Who are you speaking about?" "No, about priests..." Ah, priests are part of the Church, but the Church is all of us! Don't restrict her to priests, bishops, the Vatican...These are members of the Church, but the Church is all of us, the whole family, everyone from the mother. And the Church is a very broad reality, which is open to the whole of humanity and is not created in a laboratory, the Church is not born in a lab, she is not born suddenly. She is founded by Jesus, a people with a long history on her shoulders and a preparation that began long before Christ himself. You find the Church's history, or rather "prehistory," already in the pages of the Old Testament...

It is God himself who takes the initiative. Let us hear this: It is God himself who knocks at Abraham's door and says to him: "Go forth, leave your land, begin to walk and I will make of you a great people." And this is the beginning of the Church and within this people Jesus is born. God takes the initiative and turns his word to man, creating a bond and a new relationship with him. "But, Father, how can this be? God speaks to us?" "Yes." "And we can speak to God?" "Yes." "But can we have a conversation with God?" "Yes." This is called prayer, but it is God who started it all. Thus, God forms a people with all those who listen to his Word and set themselves on the journey, trusting in him. This is the only condition: to trust in God. If you trust in God, listen to him, and set out on the journey, this is building the Church...

—General Audience, June 18, 2014

We are not isolated and we are not Christians on an individual basis, each one on his or her own; no, *our Christian identity is to belong*! We are Christians because we belong to the Church. It is like a last name: if the first name is "I am Christian," the last name is "I belong to the Church." It is so beautiful to observe how this belonging is also expressed in the name God gives to himself. In answer to Moses in that wonderful episode of the "burning bush," he defines himself as *the God of the fathers* (cf. Ex 3:15). He doesn't say: I am the Omnipotent One..., No: *I am the God of Abraham, the God of Isaac, the God of Jacob*. In this way he reveals himself as the God who made an alliance with our fathers and remains ever faithful to his pact, who calls us to enter into this relationship which precedes us. God's relationship with his people precedes us all, it comes from that time.

—General Audience, June 25, 2014

No one becomes Christian on his or her own! Is that clear? No one becomes Christian by him- or herself. Christians are not made in a laboratory. A Christian is part of a people who comes from afar. The Christian belongs to a people called the Church and this Church is what makes him or her Christian, on the day of baptism, and then in the course of catechesis, and so on. But no one, no one becomes Christian on his or her own. If we believe, if we know how to pray, if we acknowledge the Lord and can listen to his Word, if we feel him close to us and recognize him in our brothers and sisters, it is because others, before us, lived the faith and then transmitted it to us.

—General Audience, June 25, 2014

I always remember the face of the nun who taught me the Catechism, but she always comes to mind—she is in Heaven for sure, because she was a holy woman—I always remember her and give thanks to God for this sister. Or it could be the face of the parish priest, of another priest or a sister or a catechist, who transmitted the contents of the faith to us and helped us to grow as Christians . . . So, this is the Church: one great family, where we are welcomed and learn to live as believers and disciples of the Lord Jesus . . . In the Church there is no "do it yourself," there are no "free agents."

—General Audience, June 25, 2014

 *For further reflection: Are there people who make the Church a family for me?*

Mother Church

The Church's activity and mission is an expression of her motherhood. For she is like a mother who tenderly holds Jesus and gives him to everyone with joy and generosity. No manifestation of Christ, even the most mystical, can ever be detached from the flesh and blood of the Church, from the historical concreteness of the Body of Christ. Without the Church, Jesus Christ ends up as an idea, a moral teaching, a feeling. Without the Church, our relationship with Christ would be at the mercy of our imagination, our interpretations, our moods.

Dear brothers and sisters! *Jesus Christ is the blessing* for every man and woman, and for all of humanity. The Church, in giving us Jesus, offers us the fullness of the Lord's blessing. This is precisely the mission of the people of God: to spread to all peoples God's blessing made flesh in Jesus Christ. And Mary, the first and most perfect disciple of Jesus, the first and most perfect believer, the model of the pilgrim Church, is the one who opens the way to the Church's motherhood and constantly sustains her maternal mission to all mankind. Mary's tactful maternal witness has accompanied the Church from the beginning. She, the Mother of God, is also the Mother of the Church, and through the Church, the mother of all men and women, and of every people. May this gentle and loving Mother obtain for us the Lord's blessing upon the entire human family.

—*Sermon for the Solemnity of Mary, Mother of God, January 1, 2015*

The Church is mother. The conception of Jesus in Mary's womb, in fact, is the prelude to the birth of every Christian in the womb of the Church. From the moment that Christ is the firstborn among many brethren (cf. Rom 8:29) and our first brother Jesus was born of Mary, he is the model, and we are all born of the Church.

We understand, then, how the relationship which unites Mary and the Church is so deep: by looking at Mary, we discover the most beautiful and most tender face of the Church; and by looking at the Church, we recognize the sublime features of Mary. We Christians are not orphans, we have a mama, we have a mother, and this is great! We are not orphans! The Church is mother, Mary is mother.

The Church is our mother because she has given birth to us in baptism. Each time we baptize a baby, he or she becomes a child of the Church, who enters the Church. And from that day, like an attentive mama, she helps us grow in faith and she shows us, with the strength of the Word of God, the path of salvation, defending us from harm.

—*General Audience, September 3, 2014*

The Church conducts herself like Jesus. She does not teach theoretical lessons on love, on mercy. She does not spread to the world a philosophy, a way of wisdom . . . Of course, Christianity is also all of this, but as an effect, by reflex. Mother Church, like Jesus, teaches by example, and the words serve to illuminate the meaning of her actions. Mother Church teaches us to give food and drink to those who are hungry and thirsty, to clothe those who are naked. And how does she do this? She does it through the example of so many saints, men and women, who did this in an exemplary fashion; but she does it also through the example of so many dads and mamas, who teach their children that what we have extra is for those who lack the basic necessities. It is important to know this. The rule of hospitality has always been sacred in the simplest Christian families: there is always a plate and a bed for the one in need.

—*General Audience, September 10, 2014*

Holy and Catholic

Every time we renew our profession of faith by reciting the "Creed," we affirm that the Church is "one" and "holy." She is *one,* because her origin is in the Triune God, the mystery of unity and full communion. The Church, then, is *holy,* as she is founded by Jesus Christ, enlivened by the Holy Spirit, showered with his love and his salvation. At the same time, however, she is holy and made up of sinners, all of us, sinners, who experience our fragility and our misery every day. Thus, this faith which we profess urges us toward conversion, to have the courage to live unity and holiness daily, and if we are not united, if we are not holy, it is because we are not faithful to Jesus. But he, Jesus, does not leave us on our own, He does not abandon his Church! He walks with us, He understands us. He understands our weaknesses, our sins, he forgives us always, if we let him forgive us. He is always with us, helping us to become less sinful, more holy, more united.

—*General Audience, August 27, 2014*

Once, in another diocese I had before, I heard an interesting and kind comment. It was about an older woman who had worked all her life in the parish, and a person who knew her well said: "This woman never criticized, she never gossiped, she always wore a smile." A woman like this could be canonized tomorrow! This is a good example. And if we look at the history of the Church, there are so many divisions among us Christians. Even now we are divided. Also in history, we Christians have made war among ourselves for theological differences. Let us think of the Thirty Years' War. But, this is not Christian . . . God, instead, wants us to develop the capacity to welcome, to forgive and to love each other, to be ever more like him, who is communion and love. The Church's holiness consists in this: in recognizing herself in God's image, showered with his mercy and his grace.

—General Audience, August 27, 2014

When we profess our faith, we affirm that the Church is *catholic* and *apostolic*. . . *Catholic* means universal. A complete and clear definition is offered by one of the fathers of the Church of the first centuries, Saint Cyril of Jerusalem, when he affirmed: The Church is doubtless "called catholic, meaning universal, because it extends over all the world, from one end of the earth to the other; and because it teaches universally and completely one and all the truths which ought to come to men's knowledge, concerning things both visible and invisible, heavenly and earthly" (*The Catechesis* 18:23).

A clear sign of the catholicity of the Church is that she speaks all languages, and this is the very effect of Pentecost (cf. Acts 2:1–13): the Holy Spirit, in fact, enabled the apostles and the whole Church to cause the good news of God's salvation and love to spread to all, even to the ends of the earth.

Thus, the Church was born catholic, that is, "symphonic" from her very origins, and can be only catholic, projected to evangelization and encounter with all. The Word of God can be read today in all languages; everyone has the gospel in his or her own language in order to read it.

—General Audience, September 17, 2014

When we say that the Church was born catholic, that is to say that she was born "outward-bound," that she was born missionary. Had the apostles remained in the upper room, without going out to disseminate the gospel, the Church would be the Church of only that people, of that city, of that upper room. But they all went out into the world, from the moment of the Church's birth, from the moment the Spirit descended upon them. And this is why the Church was born "outward-bound," that is, missionary.

This is what we express by deeming her *apostolic*, because an apostle is one who spreads the good news of the resurrection of Jesus. This term reminds us that the Church, which is built on the foundation of the apostles, lives on in continuity with them. Today all of us are in continuity with that group of apostles who received the Holy Spirit and then went "out" to preach. The Church is sent to take this gospel message to all men, accompanying it with the signs of the tenderness and power of God.

—General Audience, September 17, 2014

What does it mean for our communities and for each one of us to belong to a Church which is catholic and apostolic? First of all, it means *taking the salvation of all mankind to heart*, not feeling indifferent or alien in facing the fate of so many of our brothers and sisters, but open and sympathetic toward them. It means, moreover, *having a sense of the fullness, the completeness, the harmony* of the Christian life, always rejecting partisan, unilateral positions, which close us within ourselves.

Belonging to the *apostolic* Church means being aware that our faith is anchored in the proclamation and the witness of the very apostles of Jesus—it is anchored there, it is a long chain which comes from there; and for this we always feel sent, we feel delegated, in communion with the apostles' successors, to proclaim, with the heart filled with joy, Christ and his love to all mankind. And here I would like to recall the heroic life of so very many missionaries, men and women who left their homeland in order to go to proclaim the gospel in other countries, on other continents. A Brazilian cardinal who works quite often in Amazonia was telling me that when he goes to a place, to a village or a town in Amazonia, he always goes to the cemetery where he sees the tombs of the missionaries, priests, brothers, sisters who went to preach the gospel: apostles. And he thinks: all of them could be canonized now, they left all in order to proclaim Jesus Christ.

—General Audience, September 17, 2014

Christ is the model for the Church, because the Church is his body. He is the model for all Christians, for us all. When one looks to Christ, one does not err. The gospel of Luke recounts how Jesus, having returned to Nazareth, where he grew up, entered the synagogue and read, making reference to himself, the passage from the prophet Isaiah where it is written: "The Spirit of the Lord is upon me, because he has anointed me to bring good news to the poor. He has sent me to proclaim release to the captives and recovery of sight to the blind, to set at liberty those who are oppressed, to proclaim the acceptable year of the Lord's favor" (4:18–19). Behold how Christ used his humanity—for he was also a man—to proclaim and fulfill the divine plan of redemption and salvation—because he was God; so too must it be for the Church. Through her visible reality, all that can be seen, the sacraments and witness of all us Christians, the Church is called every day to be close to every man, to begin with the one who is poor, the one who suffers, and the one who is marginalized, in such a way as to make all people feel the compassionate and merciful gaze of Jesus.

—General Audience, October 29, 2014

People of God

The image of the Church I like is that of the holy, faithful people of God. This is the definition I often use, and then there is that image from the Second Vatican Council's Dogmatic Constitution on the Church (no. 12). Belonging to a people has a strong theological value. In the history of salvation, God has saved a people. There is no full identity without belonging to a people. No one is saved alone, as an isolated individual, but God attracts us looking at the complex web of relationships that take place in the human community. God enters into this dynamic, this participation in the web of human relationships.

The people itself constitutes a subject. And the Church is the people of God on the journey through history, with joys and sorrows. Thinking with the Church, therefore, is my way of being a part of this people. And all the faithful, considered as a whole, are infallible in matters of belief, and the people display this *infallibilitas in credendo,* this infallibility in believing, through a supernatural sense of the faith of all the people walking together. This is what I understand today as the "thinking with the Church" of which Saint Ignatius speaks. When the dialogue among the people and the bishops and the pope goes down this road and is genuine, then it is assisted by the Holy Spirit. So this thinking with the Church does not concern theologians only…

How are we treating the people of God? I dream of a Church that is a mother and shepherdess. The Church's ministers must be merciful, take responsibility for the people, and accompany them like the good Samaritan, who washes, cleans, and raises up his neighbor. This is pure gospel. God is greater than sin. The structural and organizational reforms are secondary—that is, they come afterward. The first reform must be the attitude. The ministers of the gospel must be people who can warm the hearts of the people, who walk through the dark night with them, who know how to dialogue and to descend themselves into their people's night, into the darkness, but without getting lost. The people of God want pastors, not clergy acting like bureaucrats or government officials. The bishops, particularly, must be able to support the movements of God among their people with patience, so that no one is left behind. But they must also be able to accompany the flock that has a flair for finding new paths.

—*Interview with Jesuit journals, published in* America *on September 19, 2013*

Christianity is not a religion just about ideas, theology, aesthetics, commandments. We are a people who follow Jesus Christ and bear witness, who want to bear witness to Jesus Christ. And that witness sometimes leads to giving your life... Witness is always fruitful, when it occurs in daily life but also when it occurs in difficult times or when it even leads to death. The Church is a fruitful mother when she bears witness to Jesus Christ. But when the Church closes in on herself, when she thinks of herself—let's put it this way—as a university of religion with so many fine ideas, so many fine buildings, so many fine museums, so many fine things but doesn't bear witness, she becomes barren. The same goes for individual Christians. If they don't bear witness they are barren, they don't give the life they have received from Jesus Christ.

What sort of witness do I bear? Am I a Christian witness to Jesus or simply a member of a sect? Am I fruitful in bearing witness or do I remain barren because I'm not capable of letting the Holy Spirit carry me forward in my Christian vocation?

—*Morning Homily, May 6, 2014*

It is not possible "to love Christ but without the Church, to listen to Christ but not the Church, to belong to Christ but outside the Church" (Paul VI, *Evangelii Nuntiandi*). For the Church is herself God's great family, which brings Christ to us. Our faith is not an abstract doctrine or philosophy, but a vital and full relationship with a person: Jesus Christ, the only-begotten Son of God who became man, was put to death, rose from the dead to save us, and is now living in our midst. Where can we encounter him? We encounter him in the Church, in our hierarchical, Holy Mother Church. It is the Church which says today: "Behold the Lamb of God"; it is the Church which proclaims him. It is in the Church that Jesus continues to accomplish his acts of grace which are the sacraments.

—*Sermon for the Solemnity of Mary, Mother of God, January 1, 2015*

. . . The Communion of Saints

The first text cited at the beginning of this book—namely, Bergoglio's personal confession of faith—makes clear Francis's view that our deceased loved ones are now in heaven where they intercede for us, and that the Church is literally a community of those who are still living and those who are deceased Christians and exist, so to speak, with one foot already in heaven. In his personal confession of faith, formulated in his own words years before he became pope, he wrote: "I believe that papa is with God in heaven. I believe that Father Duarte is also there and praying for my priesthood." (Father Duarte was the confessor of the young Jorge Mario Bergoglio.)

In presenting the Church to the men and women of our time, the Second Vatican Council kept well in mind a fundamental truth, one we should never forget: the Church is not a static reality, inert, an end in herself, but is on a continual journey through history, toward that ultimate and marvelous end that is the Kingdom of Heaven, of which the Church on earth is the seed and the beginning (cf. Dogmatic Constitution on the Church *Lumen Gentium*, no. 5). When we turn to this horizon, we discover that our imagination falls short, hardly able to intuit the splendor of a mystery which surpasses our senses. And several questions spontaneously rise up in us: When will that final step happen? What will the new dimension which the Church enters be like? What will become of humanity then? And of creation around us? But these questions are not new. The disciples had already asked Jesus about them...: "When will this come to pass? When will the Spirit triumph over creation, over creatures, over everything...?" These are human questions, time-old questions. And we too are asking these questions.

The conciliar constitution *Gaudium et Spes*, faced with these questions that forever resonate in the hearts of men and women, states: "We do not know the time for the consummation of the earth and of humanity, nor do we know how all things will be transformed. As deformed by sin, the shape of this world will pass away; but we are taught that God is preparing a new dwelling place and a new earth where justice will abide, and whose blessedness will answer and surpass all the longings for peace which spring up in the human heart" (no. 39). This is the Church's destination: it is, as the Bible says, the "new Jerusalem," "Paradise." More than a place, it is a "state" of soul in which our deepest hopes are fulfilled in superabundance and our being, as creatures and as children of God, reach their full maturity. We will finally be clothed in the joy, peace, and love of God, completely, without any limit, and we will come face to face with him! (cf. 1 Cor 13:12). It is beautiful to think of this, to think of heaven. We will all be there together. It is beautiful, it gives strength to the soul.

In this perspective, it is good to grasp the kind of continuity and deep communion there is between the Church in heaven and that which is still a pilgrim on earth. Those who already live in the sight of God can indeed sustain us and intercede for us, pray for us. On the other hand, we too are always invited to offer up good works, prayer, and the Eucharist itself in order to alleviate the tribulation of souls still awaiting never-ending beatitude. Yes, because in the Christian perspective the distinction is not between who is dead and who is not, but between who is in Christ and who is not! This is the point of determination, what is truly decisive for our salvation and for our happiness.

At the same time, sacred scripture teaches us that the fulfillment of this marvelous plan cannot but involve everything that surrounds us and came from the heart and mind of God. The apostle Paul says it explicitly, when he says that "creation itself will be set free from its bondage to decay and obtain the glorious liberty of the children of God" (Rom 8:21). Other texts utilize the image of a "new heaven" and a "new earth" (cf. 2 Pet 3:13; Rev 21:1), in the sense that the whole universe will be renewed and will be freed once and for all from every trace of evil and from death itself. What lies ahead is the fulfillment of a transformation that in reality is already happening, beginning with the death and resurrection of Christ. Hence, it is the new creation; it is not, therefore, the annihilation of the cosmos and of everything around us, but the bringing of all things into the fullness of being, of truth and of beauty. This is the design that God, the Father, Son, and Holy Spirit, willed from eternity to realize and is realizing.

Dear friends, when we think of this magnificent reality awaiting us, we become aware of how marvelous a gift it is to belong to the Church which bears in writing the highest of vocations! So, let us ask the Virgin Mary, Mother of the Church, to keep constant watch over our journey and to help us to be, as she is, a joyful sign of trust and of hope among our brothers and sisters.

—General Audience, November 26, 2014

... The Forgiveness of Sins

Here we present a theme which lies especially close to the heart of the Argentinian pope. We are all sinners, but God out of mercy will never become weary of forgiving us. This is a thought that Francis continually reiterates. He began his pontificate with this message, as the following texts show.

Jesus has this message for us: mercy. I think—and I say it with humility—that this is the Lord's most powerful message: mercy. It was he himself who said: "I did not come for the righteous." The righteous justify themselves. Go on, then, even if you can do it, I cannot! But they believe they can. "I came for sinners" (Mk 2:17).

Think of the gossip after the call of Matthew: he associates with sinners! (cf. Mk 2:16). He comes for us, when we recognize that we are sinners. But if we are like the Pharisee before the altar who said: "I thank you Lord, that I am not like other men, and especially not like the one at the door, like that publican" (cf. Lk 18:11–12), then we do not know the Lord's heart, and we will never have the joy of experiencing this mercy! It is not easy to entrust oneself to God's mercy, because it is an abyss beyond our comprehension. But we must! "Oh, Father, if you knew my life, you would not say that to me!" "Why, what have you done?" "Oh, I am a great sinner!" "All the better! Go to Jesus: he likes you to tell him these things!" He forgets, he has a very special capacity for forgetting. He forgets, he kisses you, he embraces you and he simply says to you: "Neither do I condemn you; go, and sin no more" (Jn 8:11). That is the only advice he gives you. After a month, if we are in the same situation... Let us go back to the Lord. The Lord never tires of forgiving—never! It is we who tire of asking his forgiveness. Let us ask for the grace not to tire of asking forgiveness, because he never tires of forgiving. Let us ask for this grace.

—*Sermon for the Fifth Sunday of Lent, March 17, 2013*

What a beautiful truth of faith this is for our lives: the mercy of God! God's love for us is so great, so deep; it is an unfailing love, one which always takes us by the hand and supports us, lifts us up and leads us on.

—*Sermon for Divine Mercy Sunday, April 7, 2013*

Brothers and sisters, let us never lose trust in the patience and mercy of God! Let us think too of the two disciples on the way to Emmaus: their sad faces, their barren journey, their despair. But Jesus does not abandon them: he walks beside them, and not only that! Patiently he explains the scriptures which spoke of him, and he stays to share a meal with them. This is God's way of doing things: he is not impatient like us, who often want everything all at once, even in our dealings with other people. God is patient with us because he loves us, and those who love are able to understand, to hope, to inspire confidence; they do not give up, they do not burn bridges, they are able to forgive. Let us remember this in our lives as Christians: God always waits for us, even when we have left him behind! He is never far from us, and if we return to him, he is ready to embrace us.

—Sermon for Divine Mercy Sunday, April 7, 2013

I am always struck when I reread the parable of the merciful father; it impresses me because it always gives me great hope. Think of that younger son who was in the father's house, who was loved; and yet he wants his part of the inheritance; he goes off, spends everything, hits rock bottom, where he could not be more distant from the father, yet when he is at his lowest, he misses the warmth of the father's house and he goes back. And the father? Had he forgotten the son? No, never. He is there, he sees the son from afar, he was waiting for him every hour of every day, the son was always in his father's heart, even though he had left him, even though he had squandered his whole inheritance, his freedom. The father, with patience, love, hope, and mercy, had never for a second stopped thinking about him, and as soon as he sees him still far off, he runs out to meet him and embraces him with tenderness, the tenderness of God, without a word of reproach: he has returned! And that is the joy of the father. In that embrace for his son is all this joy: he has returned! God is always waiting for us, he never grows tired. Jesus shows us this merciful patience of God so that we can regain confidence, hope—always! A great German theologian, Romano Guardini, said that God responds to our weakness by his patience, and this is the reason for our confidence, our hope... It is like a dialogue between our weakness and the patience of God, it is a dialogue that, if we do it, will grant us hope.

—*Sermon for Divine Mercy Sunday, April 7, 2013*

God's patience has to call forth in us the courage to return to him, however many mistakes and sins there may be in our life. Jesus tells Thomas to put his hand in the wounds of his hands and his feet, and in his side. We too can enter into the wounds of Jesus, we can actually touch him. This happens every time that we receive the sacraments with faith. Saint Bernard, in a fine homily, says: "Through the wounds of Jesus I can suck honey from the rock and oil from the flinty rock (cf. Deut 32:13), I can taste and see the goodness of the Lord" (*On the Song of Songs*, 61:4). It is there, in the wounds of Jesus, that we are truly secure; there we encounter the boundless love of his heart. Thomas understood this. Saint Bernard goes on to ask: But what can I count on? My own merits? No, "My merit is God's mercy. I am by no means lacking merits as long as he is rich in mercy. If the mercies of the Lord are manifold, I too will abound in merits" (ibid., 61:5). This is important: the courage to trust in Jesus' mercy, to trust in his patience, to seek refuge always in the wounds of his love. Saint Bernard even states: "So what if my conscience gnaws at me for my many sins? 'Where sin has abounded, there grace has abounded all the more' (Rom 5:20)" (ibid.).

—*Sermon for Divine Mercy Sunday, April 7, 2013*

Maybe someone among us here is thinking: my sin is so great, I am as far from God as the younger son in the parable, my unbelief is like that of Thomas; I don't have the courage to go back, to believe that God can welcome me and that he is waiting for me, of all people. But God is indeed waiting for you; he asks of you only the courage to go to him. How many times in my pastoral ministry have I heard it said: "Father, I have many sins"; and I have always pleaded: "Don't be afraid, go to him, he is waiting for you, he will take care of everything." We hear many offers from the world around us, but let us take up God's offer instead: his is a caress of love. For God, we are not numbers, we are important, indeed we are the most important thing to him; even if we are sinners, we are what is closest to his heart.

—*Sermon for Divine Mercy Sunday, April 7, 2013*

Jesus took on our nakedness, he took upon himself the shame of Adam, the nakedness of his sin, in order to wash away our sin: by his wounds we have been healed.

Remember what Saint Paul says: "What shall I boast of, if not my weakness, my poverty?" Precisely in feeling my sinfulness, in looking at my sins, I can see and encounter God's mercy, his love, and go to him to receive forgiveness.

In my own life, I have so often seen God's merciful countenance, his patience; I have also seen so many people find the courage to enter the wounds of Jesus by saying to him: Lord, I am here, accept my poverty, hide my sin in your wounds, wash it away with your blood. And I have always seen that God did just this—he accepted them, consoled them, cleansed them, loved them.

Dear brothers and sisters, let us be enveloped by the mercy of God; let us trust in his patience, which always gives us more time. Let us find the courage to return to his house, to dwell in his loving wounds, allowing ourselves be loved by him and to encounter his mercy in the sacraments. We will feel his wonderful tenderness, we will feel his embrace, and we too will become more capable of mercy, patience, forgiveness, and love.

—*Sermon for Divine Mercy Sunday, April 7, 2013*

Always remember this: life is a journey. It is a path, a journey to meet Jesus. At the end, and forever. A journey in which we do not encounter Jesus is not a Christian journey. It is for the Christian to continually encounter Jesus, to watch him, to let himself be watched over by Jesus, because Jesus watches us with love; he loves us so much, he loves us so much and he is always watching over us. To encounter

Jesus also means allowing oneself to be gazed upon by him. "But, Father, you know," one of you might say to me, "you know that this journey is horrible for me, I am such a sinner, I have committed many sins . . . how can I encounter Jesus?" And you know that the people whom Jesus most sought out were the greatest sinners; and they reproached him for this, and the people—those who believed themselves righteous—would say: This is no true prophet, look what lovely company he keeps! He was with sinners . . . And he said: I came for those in need of salvation, in need of healing. Jesus heals our sins. And along the way Jesus comes and forgives us—all of us sinners, we are all sinners—even when we make a mistake, when we commit a sin, when we sin. And this forgiveness that we receive in confession is an encounter with Jesus. We always encounter Jesus.

So let us go forward in life like this, as the prophet says, to the mountain, until the day when we shall attain the final encounter, when we will be able to look upon the beautiful gaze of Jesus, it is so beautiful. This is the Christian life: to walk, to go forward, united as brothers and sisters, loving one another. Encounter Jesus. Do you agree, the nine of you? Do you want to meet Jesus in your lives? Yes? This is important in the Christian life. Today, with the seal of the Holy Spirit, you will have greater strength for the journey, for the encounter with Jesus. Take courage, do not be afraid! Life is this journey. And the most beautiful gift is to meet Jesus. Go forward, be brave!

—*Sermon for the First Sunday of Advent, December 1, 2013*

Leave the Grave

We all have within us some areas, some parts of our heart, that are not alive, that are a little dead; and some of us have many dead places in our hearts, a true spiritual necrosis! And when we are in this situation, we know it, we want to get out but we can't. Only the power of Jesus, the power of Jesus can help us come out of these atrophied zones of the heart, these tombs of sin, which we all have. We are all sinners! But if we become very attached to these tombs and guard them within us and do not will that our whole heart rise again to life, we become corrupted and our soul begins to give off, as Martha says, an "odor" (Jn 11:39), the stench of a person who is attached to sin. And Lent is something to do with this. Because all of us, who are sinners, do not end up attached to sin, but that we can hear what Jesus said to Lazarus: "He cried out with a loud voice: 'Lazarus, come out'" (Jn 11:43).

Today I invite you to think for a moment, in silence, here: Where is my interior necrosis? Where is the dead part of my soul? Where is my tomb? Think, for a short moment, all of you in silence. Let us think: What part of the heart can be corrupted because of my attachment to sin, one sin or another? And to remove the stone, to take away the stone of shame and allow the Lord to say to us, as he said to Lazarus: "Come out!" That all our soul might be healed, might be raised by the love of Jesus, by the power of Jesus. He is capable of forgiving us. We all need it! All of us. We are all sinners, but we must be careful not to become corrupt! Sinners we may be, but he forgives us. Let us hear that voice of Jesus who, by the power of God, says to us: "Come out! Leave that tomb you have within you. Come out. I give you life, I give you happiness, I bless you, I want you for myself."

—*Sermon for the Fifth Sunday of Lent, April 6, 2014*

...*The Resurrection of the Body, and Life Everlasting*

At the end of time, what will happen to the people of God? What will happen to each of us? What should we expect? The apostle Paul encouraged the Christians of the Thessalonian community, who were asking themselves these questions, and after his explanation they said these words, which are among the most beautiful of the New Testament: "And so we shall always be with the Lord"! (1 Thes 4:17). They are simple words, but laden with such great hope! "And so we shall always be with the Lord." Do you believe this?...It seems not. Do you believe? Shall we repeat it together? Three times: "And so we shall always be with the Lord." "And so we shall always be with the Lord." "And so we shall always be with the Lord." It is emblematic that John, taking up the intuition of the prophets in the book of Revelation, describes the final, definitive dimension in terms of the "new Jerusalem, coming down out of heaven from God, prepared as a bride adorned for her husband"

(Rev 21:2). That is what awaits us! This, then, is who the Church is: she is the People of God who follows the Lord Jesus and who prepares herself day by day for the meeting with him, as a bride with her bridegroom. And this is not just an expression: there will be actual nuptials! Yes, because Christ, by becoming a man like us and making us all one with him, with his death and his resurrection, truly wedded us and constituted us as a people, as his bride. This is none other than the fulfillment of the plan of communion and of love woven by God throughout history, the history of the people of God and also the very history of each one of us. It is the Lord who is in the lead.

—General Audience, October 15, 2014

There is another aspect, however, which further comforts us and which opens the heart: John tells us that in the Church, the Bride of Christ, the "new Jerusalem" is made visible. This means that the Church, in addition to bride, is called to become a city, the symbol par excellence of human coexistence and relationality. How beautiful, then, already being able to contemplate, according to another very evocative image in Revelation, all people and all peoples gathered together in this city, as in a tent, "the tent of God" (cf. Rev 21:3)! And in this glorious framework there will no longer be isolation, prevarication or distinctions of any kind—of a social, ethnic or religious nature—but we will all be one in Christ.

—General Audience, October 15, 2014

In light of this wonderful and unprecedented scene, our heart cannot help feeling strongly confirmed in hope. You see, Christian hope is not simply a desire, a wish, it is not optimism: for a Christian, hope is expectation, fervent expectation, impassioned by the ultimate and definitive fulfillment of a mystery, the mystery of God's love, in which we are born again and which are already experiencing. And it is the expectation of someone who is coming: it is Christ the Lord approaching ever closer to us, day by day, and who comes to bring us at last into the fullness of his communion and of his peace. The Church then, has the task of keeping the lamp of hope burning and clearly visible, so that it may continue to shine as a sure sign of salvation and illuminate for all humanity the path which leads to the encounter with the merciful face of God.

—General Audience, October 15, 2014

Dear brothers and sisters, here then is what we are awaiting: Jesus' return! The Church as bride awaits her Spouse! We must ask ourselves, however, with total sincerity: are we truly luminous and credible witnesses to this expectation, to this hope? Do our communities still live in the sign of the presence of the Lord Jesus and in the warm expectation of his coming, or do they appear tired, sluggish, weighed down by fatigue and resignation? Do we too run the risk of exhausting the oil of faith, and the oil of joy? Let us be careful!

Let us invoke the Virgin Mary, Mother of Hope and Queen of Heaven, that she may always keep us alert, listening and expectant, so that we may, already now, be permeated by Christ's love and take part one day in the unending joy, in the full communion of God. Always remember, never forget: "And so we shall always be with the Lord!" (1 Thes 4:17).

—General Audience, October 15, 2014

The vision of Heaven . . . is very beautiful: the Lord God, beauty, goodness, truth, tenderness, love in its fullness. All of this awaits us. Those who have gone before us and who have died in the Lord are there. They proclaim that they have been saved not through their own works, though good works they surely did, but that they have been saved by the Lord: "Salvation belongs to our God who sits upon the throne, and to the Lamb!" (Rev 7:10). It is he who saves us, it is he who at the end of our lives takes us by the hand like a father, precisely to that heaven where our ancestors are. One of the elders asks: "Who are these, clothed in white robes, and whence have they come?" (v. 13). Who are these righteous ones, these saints who are in heaven? The reply is: "These are they who have come out of the great tribulation; they have washed their robes and made them white in the blood of the Lamb" (v. 14).

—Sermon for the Solemnity of All Saints, November 1, 2013

Our Anchor: Hope

This is the Lord's blessing that we still have: hope. Hope that he will have mercy on his people, pity on those who are in great tribulation, and compassion for the destroyers so that they will convert. And so, the holiness of the Church goes on: with these people, with us, that we will see God as he is. What should our attitude be if we want to be part of this multitude journeying to the Father, in this world of devastation, in this world of war, in this world of tribulation? Our attitude, as we heard in the gospel, is the attitude of the beatitudes. That path alone will lead us to the encounter with God. That path alone will save us from destruction, from destroying the earth, creation, morality, history, family, everything. That path alone. But it too will bring us through bad things! It will bring us problems, persecution. But that path alone will take us forward. And so, these people who are suffering so much today because of the selfishness of destroyers, of our brothers' destroyers, these people struggle onward with the beatitudes, with the hope of finding God, of coming face-to-face with the Lord in the hope of becoming saints, at the moment of our final encounter with him.

May the Lord help us and give us the grace of this hope, but also the grace of courage to emerge from all this destruction, devastation, the relativism of life, the exclusion of others, exclusion of values, exclusion of all that the Lord has given us: the exclusion of peace. May he deliver us from this, and give us the grace to walk in the hope of finding ourselves one day face-to-face with him. And this hope, brothers and sisters, does not disappoint!

—Sermon for the Solemnity of All Saints, November 1, 2013

The first Christians depicted hope with an anchor, as though life were an anchor cast on heaven's shores and all of us journeying to that shore, clinging to the anchor's rope. This is a beautiful image of hope: to have our hearts anchored there, where our beloved predecessors are, where the saints are, where Jesus is, where God is. This is the hope that does not disappoint; today and tomorrow are days of hope.

Hope is a little like leaven that expands our souls. There are difficult moments in life, but with hope the soul goes forward and looks ahead to what awaits us.

—Sermon for the Solemnity of All Saints, November 1, 2013

Today...each one of us can think of the twilight of life: "What will my passing away be like?" All of us will experience sundown, all of us! Do we look at it with hope? Do we look with that joy at being welcomed by the Lord? This is a Christian thought that gives us hope. Today is a day of joy; however it is serene and tranquil joy, a peaceful joy. Let us think about the passing away of so many of our brothers and sisters who have preceded us, let us think about the evening of our life, when it will come. And let us think about our hearts and ask ourselves: "Where is my heart anchored?" If it is not firmly anchored, let us anchor it beyond, on that shore, knowing that hope does not disappoint because the Lord Jesus does not disappoint.

—Sermon for the Solemnity of All Saints, November 1, 2013

For further reflection: Where is my heart "anchored"?

Selections from Lumen Fidei

That the first encyclical of Pope Francis reflects on the theme of Christian faith was accidental. Pope Benedict XVI had prepared the text to coincide with the "Year of Faith," but he could not finish this text before his retirement in February 2013. His successor Pope Francis took up the text, supplemented it, wrote parts of it, and published it. In the encyclical it is difficult to differentiate between what came from the pen of Pope Benedict and what came from the pen of Pope Francis. In any case, Francis made this text his own, and therefore one may read the entire text as from him and by him.

4. Faith is born of an encounter with the living God who calls us and reveals his love, a love which precedes us and upon which we can lean for security and for building our lives. Transformed by this love, we gain fresh vision, new eyes to see; we realize that it contains a great promise of fulfillment, and that a vision of the future opens up before us. Faith, received from God as a supernatural gift, becomes a light for our way, guiding our journey through time.

7. In God's gift of faith, a supernatural infused virtue, we realize that a great love has been offered us, a good word has been spoken to us, and that when we welcome that word, Jesus Christ the Word made flesh, the Holy Spirit transforms us, lights up our way to the future and enables us joyfully to advance along that way on wings of hope. Thus wonderfully interwoven, faith, hope, and charity are the driving force of the Christian life as it advances toward full communion with God. But what is it like, this road which faith opens up before us? What is the origin of this powerful light which brightens the journey of a successful and fruitful life?

8. Faith is linked to hearing. Abraham does not see God, but hears his voice. Faith thus takes on a personal aspect. God is not the god of a particular place, or a deity linked to specific sacred time, but the God of a person, the God of Abraham, Isaac, and Jacob, capable of interacting with man and establishing a covenant with him. Faith is our response to a word which engages us personally, to a "Thou" who calls us by name.

21. We come to see the difference, then, which faith makes for us. Those who believe are transformed by the love to which they have opened their hearts in faith. By their openness to this offer of primordial love, their lives are enlarged and expanded...The Christian can see with the eyes of Jesus and share in his mind, his filial disposition, because he or she shares in his love, which is the Spirit. In the love of Jesus, we receive in a certain way his vision.

22. Those who believe come to see themselves in the light of the faith which they profess: Christ is the mirror in which they find their own image fully realized.

24. We need knowledge, we need truth, because without these we cannot stand firm, we cannot move forward. Faith without truth does not save, it does not provide a sure footing. It remains a beautiful story, the projection of our deep yearning for happiness, something capable of satisfying us to the extent that we are willing to deceive ourselves. Either that, or it is reduced to a lofty sentiment which brings consolation and cheer, yet remains prey to the vagaries of our spirit and the changing seasons, incapable of sustaining a steady journey through life.

26. Faith transforms the whole person precisely to the extent that he or she becomes open to love. Through this blending of faith and love we come to see the kind of knowledge which faith entails, its power to convince and its ability to illumine our steps.

28. The true God is the God of fidelity who keeps his promises and makes possible, in time, a deeper understanding of his plan.

34. One who believes may not be presumptuous; on the contrary, truth leads to humility, since believers know that, rather than ourselves possessing truth, it is truth which embraces and possesses us. Far from making us inflexible, the

security of faith sets us on a journey; it enables witness and dialogue with all.

35. Religious man strives to see signs of God in the daily experiences of life, in the cycle of the seasons, in the fruitfulness of the earth and in the movement of the cosmos. God is light and he can be found also by those who seek him with a sincere heart.

An image of this seeking can be seen in the Magi, who were led to Bethlehem by the star (cf. Mt 2:1–12). For them God's light appeared as a journey to be undertaken, a star which led them on a path of discovery. The star is a sign of God's patience with our eyes which need to grow accustomed to his brightness. Religious man is a wayfarer; he must be ready to let himself be led, to come out of himself and to find the God of perpetual surprises. This respect on God's part for our human eyes shows us that when we draw near to God, our human lights are not dissolved in the immensity of his light, as a star is engulfed by the dawn, but shine all the more brightly the closer they approach the primordial fire, like a mirror which reflects light. Christian faith in Jesus, the one Savior of the world, proclaims that all God's light is concentrated in him, in his "luminous life" which discloses the origin and the end of history. There is no human experience, no journey of man to God, which cannot be taken up, illumined, and purified by this light. The more Christians immerse themselves in the circle of Christ's light, the more capable they become of understanding and accompanying the path of every man and woman toward God.

Because faith is a way, it also has to do with the lives of those men and women who, though not believers, nonetheless desire to believe and continue to seek. To the extent that they are sincerely open to love and set out with whatever light they can find, they are already, even without knowing it, on the path leading to faith. They strive to act as if God existed, at times because they realize how important he is for finding a sure compass for our life in common or because they experience a desire for light amid darkness, but also because in perceiving life's grandeur and beauty they intuit that the presence of God would make it all the more beautiful... Anyone who sets off on the path of doing good to others is already drawing near to God, is already sustained by his help, for it is characteristic of the divine light to brighten our eyes whenever we walk toward the fullness of love.

39. It is impossible to believe on our own. Faith is not simply an individual decision which takes place in the depths of the believer's heart, nor a completely private relationship between the "I" of the believer and the divine "Thou," between an autonomous subject and God. By its very nature, faith is open to the "we" of the Church; it always takes place within her communion. We are reminded of this by the dialogical format of the Creed used in the baptismal liturgy. Our belief is expressed in response to an invitation, to a word which

must be heard and which is not my own; it exists as part of a dialogue and cannot be merely a profession originating in an individual. We can respond in the singular—"I believe"—only because we are part of a greater fellowship, only because we also say "We believe" . . .

Those who receive faith discover that their horizons expand as new and enriching relationships come to life.

40. The Church, like every family, passes on to her children the whole store of her memories . . . For transmitting a purely doctrinal content, an idea might suffice, or perhaps a book, or the repetition of a spoken message. But what is communicated in the Church, what is handed down in her living Tradition, is the new light born of an encounter with the true God, a light which touches us at the core of our being and engages our minds, wills, and emotions, opening us to relationships lived in communion. There is a special means for passing down this fullness, a means capable of engaging the entire person, body and spirit, interior life and relationships with others. It is the sacraments, celebrated in the Church's liturgy. The sacraments communicate an incarnate memory, linked to the times and places of our lives, linked to all our senses; in them the whole person is engaged as a member of a living subject and part of a network of communitarian relationships.

45. In the celebration of the sacraments, the Church hands down her memory especially through the profession of faith. The Creed does not only involve giving one's assent

to a body of abstract truths; rather, when it is recited the whole of life is drawn into a journey toward full communion with the living God. We can say that in the Creed believers are invited to enter into the mystery which they profess and to be transformed by it. To understand what this means, let us look first at the contents of the Creed. It has a trinitarian structure: the Father and the Son are united in the Spirit of love. The believer thus states that the core of all being, the inmost secret of all reality, is the divine communion. The Creed also contains a christological confession: it takes us through all the mysteries of Christ's life up to his death, resurrection, and ascension into heaven before his final return in glory. It tells us that this God of communion, reciprocal love between the Father and the Son in the Spirit, is capable of embracing all of human history and drawing it into the dynamic unity of the Godhead, which has its source and fulfillment in the Father. The believer who professes his or her faith is taken up, as it were, into the truth being professed. He or she cannot truthfully recite the words of the Creed without being changed, without becoming part of that history of love which embraces us and expands our being, making it part of a great fellowship, the ultimate subject which recites the Creed, namely, the Church. All the truths in which we believe point to the mystery of the new life of faith as a journey of communion with the living God.

51. Faith is truly a good for everyone; it is a common good. Its light does not simply brighten the interior of the Church,

nor does it serve solely to build an eternal city in the hereafter; it helps us build our societies in such a way that they can journey toward a future of hope.

54. Faith teaches us to see that every man and woman represents a blessing for me, that the light of God's face shines on me through the faces of my brothers and sisters.

55. Could it be the case, instead, that we are the ones who are ashamed to call God our God? That we are the ones who fail to confess him as such in our public life, who fail to propose the grandeur of the life in common which he makes possible? Faith illumines life and society. If it possesses a creative light for each new moment of history, it is because it sets every event in relationship to the origin and destiny of all things in the Father.

56. Christians know that suffering cannot be eliminated, yet it can have meaning and become an act of love and entrustment into the hands of God who does not abandon us; in this way it can serve as a moment of growth in faith and love. By contemplating Christ's union with the Father even at the height of his suffering on the cross (cf. Mk 15:34), Christians learn to share in the same gaze of Jesus. Even death is illumined and can be experienced as the ultimate call to faith, the ultimate "Go forth from your land" (Gen 12:1), the ultimate "Come!" spoken by the Father, to whom we abandon ourselves in the confidence that he will keep us steadfast even in our final passage.

57. Faith is not a light which scatters all our darkness, but a lamp which guides our steps in the night and suffices for the journey. To those who suffer, God does not provide arguments which explain everything; rather, his response is that of an accompanying presence, a history of goodness which touches every story of suffering and opens up a ray of light. In Christ, God himself wishes to share this path with us and to offer us his gaze so that we might see the light within it.